Cupcake heaven

Cupcake heaven

Hundreds of divine recipes to take you to baking paradise

Edited by **JENNIE MILSOM**

METRO BOOKS
New York

METRO BOOKS
New York

An imprint of Sterling Publishing
387 Park Avenue South
New York, NY 10016

This book was conceived, designed, and produced by
Quintet Publishing Limited
6 Blundell Street
London N7 9BH
United Kingdom
QTT.CCHE

Project Editor: Martha Burley
Editorial Assistant: Carly Beckerman-Boys
Designers: Susi Martin, Chris Taylor
Food Stylist: Liz Martin
Photographer: Michael Dannenberg
Art Editors: Zoë White, Jane Laurie
Art Director: Michael Charles
Managing Editor: Donna Gregory
Publisher: Mark Searle

ISBN: 978-1-4351-2250-5

Manufactured in China

4 6 8 10 9 7 5 3

www.sterlingpublishing.com

CONTENTS

Introduction

The basic cupcake is a simple thing—flour, sugar, butter, and eggs, baked in a muffin pan. Yet they've taken the baking world by storm, and it's hard to think of a dessert or sweet snack more likely to make people's eyes light up with hunger. Maybe it's the handy individual portion size, or the memories of childhood treats they stir up; more likely, it's the fact that they offer endless scope for creative decoration, embellishment, and frosting, using whichever colors and patterns you feel like. Almost 200 recipes are given in this book, showing a huge range of cakemaking techniques and decoration ideas. First, read through the following pages for advice on the basic principles of baking, which will stand you in good stead for the recipes that follow.

Equipment

No specialty equipment is required to make a batch of sweet, fluffily light cupcakes, but there are a few basic kitchen tools you'll want to have on hand to make baking as straightforward as possible.

Weighing and measuring

Successful baking depends on measuring the proportions of different ingredients correctly, to make sure your batter is neither too wet nor too stiff and dry. Accurate scales are essential, or good-quality measuring cups, spoons, and pitchers if you prefer to measure ingredients by volume.

Preparing the batter

You'll need at least one large mixing bowl to prepare the batter, along with a smaller bowl to mix the ingredients for frostings. Use heatproof glass bowls where possible—you can soften butter and melt chocolate in these.

Baking

Muffin pans have molds that are just the right size for baking cupcakes. Use nonstick ones for preference, as it's much easier to remove the cooked cakes neatly. You might want to use baking cups, too. Traditionally these are made of foil or paper; they're usually pleated, and often brightly patterned. Reusable silicon cups are more expensive to start with, but they can be used time and again.

Investing in a digital timer, or using the timer on your oven, will also save burning the batter and wasting your work.

Other equipment

Wire racks for cooling the finished cakes are essential; leaving them in the pan too long while they cool will result in heavy, overcooked cupcakes. An electric mixer makes beating and whisking the batter the work of moments— freestanding ones are readily available, though handheld versions are less expensive. Finally, a pastry brush helps when glazing decorations with egg white for a shiny finish, or when making crystallized flowers.

Ingredients

The four basic ingredients of any cupcake—fat, flour, sugar, and eggs—can be varied as you wish to suit different tastes and varying dietary needs.

Fat
Softened sweet butter is the fat of choice for cupcake making. It gives a rich, pleasant flavor and light golden color to the cakes. Avoid salted butter when baking sweet things. Margarine and flavorless vegetable-based fats are readily available in supermarkets, and can be used in cupcakes—particularly useful if you have a dairy allergy or prefer to use lower-fat products—but they will not give the same rich flavor and texture as butter. Whichever fat you choose, remember to remove it from the refrigerator a couple of hours before baking so that it is easy to work with.

Flour
All-purpose flour is the most commonly used type of flour for cupcakes, though you will need to add a leavening agent to make the cakes light and risen. The leavening agent could be baking powder, or it could be a combination of baking soda with an acidic liquid (e.g. buttermilk). Self-rising flour (which has the leavening agent

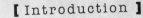

already added) can also be used. To make your own self-rising flour, sift together 6 cups all-purpose flour, 3 tablespoons baking powder, and 1 tablespoon salt. Store in an airtight container until ready to use. Wholewheat flour adds a dense texture and is rarely suitable for use when making cupcakes. You could experiment with the use of non-wheat flours and ground nuts if you do not eat wheat—ground almonds, in particular, make a light, moist cupcake.

Sugar

Regular granulated sugar can be used when making cupcakes, but you will get a better result using superfine sugar (try making your own by simply whizzing granulated sugar in a food processor). Brown sugars add a hint of caramel color and fudgelike flavor as well as sweetness, as do honey or maple syrup.

Eggs

Recipes in this book use large eggs unless otherwise stated; and free range eggs are recommended.

11

Baking advice

Before you start making the batter, remember to grease your pan, even if it should be nonstick. You could brush vegetable oil or melted butter into the molds, or use nonstick parchment paper, or use baking cups. This will save a lot of time and frustration when trying to prise your freshly baked cupcakes from their molds.

Start with all ingredients at room temperature. Fat will be easier to beat in when slightly softened; and eggs, in particular, should be removed from the referigerator an hour or two before you use them.

The two basic methods called for in this book are whisking—where you whisk the eggs and sugar together, then fold in the dry ingredients—and creaming, which means beating together fat and sugar, then the eggs, and finally folding in the flour. In both cases the aim is obviously to mix the ingredients but, crucially, to add air. The tiny air bubbles you introduce with your whisk or wooden spoon will expand when heated in the oven, giving the light, spongy texture you are aiming for.

The oven temperatures given in this book are as accurate as possible, but remember that every oven is different. Be prepared to adjust the temperature slightly if the cupcakes seem to be cooking more quickly or more slowly than the recipe implies.

(2.26 kg)

The best way to tell if a cupcake is cooked through is by inserting a metal skewer or knife into the center. If it comes out clean, it's cooked; if batter sticks to the knife, keep on cooking and check again a few minutes later. Finished cupcakes should look well risen and feel firm yet springy to the touch.

Your finished and cooled cupcakes can be stored in an airtight container for a couple of days. They'll stale slightly after that, but will still be good for another day or two. It's best to frost only on the day of serving, where possible, as frostings based on fresh cream, cream cheese, and other dairy produce really can't be kept at room temperature for more than a few hours.

Cooked cupcakes can also be frozen, in an airtight container, for up to three months before being defrosted and baked. And you can even freeze uncooked cupcake batter for up to six weeks, again provided that you seal it in an airtight container.

Frostings

Cream

The simplest frosting you can use is heavy cream, whisked until firm, sweetened to taste, and flavored with citrus zest, vanilla extract, rosewater, orange flower water, honey, or liqueurs. Do use heavy cream, not whipping cream, which will be less firm and is likely to spill over the sides of the cakes.

Fondant

Fondant frosting can be bought in white blocks. It's easy to make it in different colors—just tear off a section, add a couple of drops of food coloring, and knead so that the coloring is dispersed. It can also be formed into three-dimensional shapes like flowers and animals, or rolled out and stamped with cookie cutters into stars, leaves, and other shapes.

Glace frosting

To make a simple glace frosting, pour 2 tablespoons of boiling water over 1½ cups sifted confectioner's sugar. Mix together and frost the cakes quickly before the frosting sets. Again, you can vary this by adding food coloring, or by replacing the water with freshly squeezed lemon juice or strong black coffee. For a chocolate version, replace 2 tablespoons of the sugar with the same amount of unsweetened cocoa powder.

Buttercream

Beat ½ cup butter until light and fluffy, then beat in 2 cups sifted confectioner's sugar a little at a time until well mixed. If wished, beat in either 1 large egg yolk or 2 tablespoons milk to give a richer, glossy frosting.

Chocolate ganache

Heat 1 cup heavy cream almost to boiling point. Remove from the heat. Break 8 ounces bittersweet chocolate into small pieces and add to the

cream. Let stand for several minutes until the chocolate has melted. Beat well, then let cool. This very rich frosting can be spread over cupcakes immediately, or whipped to lighten it and increase the volume.

Fudge frosting

This is a soft frosting that can be swirled easily to give a decorative effect. Once cold, it sets firm on the surface but remains soft underneath. To make it, heat ½ cup light cream and 1 cup sugar very gently in a saucepan until the sugar is dissolved. Increase the heat and boil the mixture for about 15 minutes, until it reaches 240°F (115°C) on a sugar thermometer. If you don't have a sugar thermometer, a small spoonful of the mixture should form a soft ball when dropped into cold water. Stir frequently to prevent the mixture sticking to the saucepan. Let cool for about 2 minutes, then beat in ½ cup sweet butter, a little at a time. If the frosting starts to look oily, add an ice cube and beat vigorously until it has melted. This will return the frosting to a good consistency.

Decorations

The easiest decoration is simply to dust a batch of cupcakes with sifted confectioner's sugar. Fresh berries—blueberries, raspberries, halved strawberries, and blackcurrants—also look attractive. Other fresh fruits could also be used; try small slices of fresh citrus fruits. Chocolates and candies, as well as brightly colored sugar sprinkles, are a great decoration for children's cupcakes. Chocolate is an ideal decoration for cupcakes that have chocolate or cocoa in the batter or frosting. Try using a vegetable peeler to make chocolate shavings, or a grater to make finer shreds. Silver and gold dragées look stunning on top of cupcakes with a chocolate ganache frosting. For a more traditional look, try sprinkling shredded dried coconut, flaked almonds, or chopped hazelnuts, walnuts, and pecans.

Classic Cupcakes

These are the essential cupcakes—the recipes no self-respecting cupcake fan can do without!

Classic Cupcakes

Classic cupcakes are recipes you can't live without, the traditional treats loved by whole families everywhere. The basic tenets of cupcake heaven, this chapter holds a mix of simple and more advanced recipes that will start or expand your cupcake repertoire. If you're new to this fine art, there are a few easy tips to make sure results are good first time.

Only fill your cases two-thirds full, any more and you'll end up with a gooey mess instead of a cupcake, any less, and they will be too small. Also be careful not to over-mix the batter. This will result in chewy cupcakes instead of that light and fluffy texture we all love so much. If you're using an electric mixer, handheld varieties are better for cupcakes because they are gentler and a little slower than stand mixers. If you bring all ingredients to room temperature before mixing, this helps everything to blend easily and avoids over-mixing.

Always test for doneness after the minimum cooking time, and only bake one batch at a time. An oven is a very personal appliance, so yours might run a little hotter or a little cooler than standard new ovens used to test the recipes. A little trial and error goes a long way to making the perfect classic cupcakes.

Vanilla Cupcakes

The grand dame of cupcakes. If you can get vanilla sugar, use half regular superfine and half vanilla superfine. This will really enhance the vanilla flavor.

1 cup (2 sticks) sweet butter, softened
1 cup superfine sugar
1 tsp. vanilla extract
5 large eggs
2 cups sifted all-purpose flour
3 tsp. baking powder

Preheat the oven to 325°F (160°C). Place 18 paper baking cups muffin pans.

Cream butter, sugar, and vanilla together until light and fluffy (approximately 2 minutes with an electric beater, or 4–5 minutes by hand). Gently beat in the eggs one at a time, adding a tablespoon of the flour if the mix starts to separate. Fold in the flour and baking powder until just mixed. Pour mix into baking cups and bake for 20 minutes.

Remove the pans from the oven and cool for 5 minutes, then remove the cupcakes and cool on a rack. Store in an airtight container for up to 3 days, or freeze for up to 3 months.

Makes 1½ **dozen**

TIP

Add a couple of tablespoons of golden raisins or chocolate chips for an easy variation on this classic recipe.

Orange & Lemon Syrup Cupcakes

Make these sticky cupcakes ahead of time to let the syrup soak through.

For the cupcakes
2 medium, seedless sweet oranges,
    peeled and roughly chopped (peel
    reserved for syrup)
rind and juice of 1 lemon
½ cup (1 stick) sweet butter
1 cup superfine sugar
2 extra-large eggs
½ cup semolina
½ cup ground almond
½ cup all-purpose flour
½ tsp. baking powder

For the syrup
peel of 1 orange from
    cupcake recipe
peel of 1 lemon
½ cup superfine sugar
1 cup water

TIP
You could try replacing
an orange with half of a
medium grapefruit and
using the rind too for
a bitter citrus twist on
the recipe.

Preheat the oven to 325°F (160°C). Place 18 paper baking cups
in muffin pans.

In a saucepan, cover the oranges with water. Simmer
until tender, about 15 minutes. Cool. Drain the oranges
and purée in a food processor with the lemon juice. In
a bowl, beat the butter and sugar with an electric mixer
until light. Slowly beat in the eggs. Stir in the rest of the
ingredients, along with the orange purée, until well
combined. Spoon the mixture into the cups. Bake for
35 minutes. Remove pan from the oven and cool.

To make the syrup, thinly slice the orange and lemon
rinds, removing the pith. In a pan, bring the sugar and
water to a simmer, stirring to dissolve the sugar. Add
the orange and lemon peel and boil uncovered for
5 minutes, or until tender. Spoon the syrup onto each
cupcake. Store in an airtight container for up
to 2 days.

Makes 1½ **dozen**

Hummingbird Cupcakes

The hummingbird cake is a classic recipe from the American South.

For the cupcakes
1¼ cups all-purpose flour
1 tsp. baking powder
½ tsp. cinnamon
¾ cup superfine sugar
½ cup safflower oil
2 extra-large eggs
½ cup (2 medium) mashed bananas
1½ tbsp. grated orange zest
½ cup shredded carrot
½ cup crushed pineapple, drained
½ cup (2 oz) flaked coconut

For the frosting
½ cup (1 stick) sweet butter, softened
2½ cups confectioners' sugar, sifted
2 tbsp. freshly squeezed orange juice
2 tbsp. orange marmalade

TIP
Replacing this frosting with a lemon-flavored one works well—see page 30.

Preheat the oven to 350°F (175°C). Place 12 baking cups in a muffin pan.

In a medium bowl, sift the flour, baking powder, and cinnamon. In a large bowl cream the sugar and oil with an electric mixer until light and fluffy. Beat in the eggs slowly, then stir in the dry ingredients in 3 batches. Add the rest of the ingredients, and stir until combined. Spoon the batter into the cups. Bake for 25 minutes. Remove pan from the oven and cool for 5 minutes. Then remove the cupcakes and cool on a rack.

To make the frosting, beat the butter in a medium bowl. Add the remaining ingredients. Smear the frosting onto the cupcakes. Store unfrosted in an airtight container for up to 3 days, or freeze for up to 3 months.

Makes 1 dozen

Lemon Meringue Cupcakes

This is an unusual take on the classic lemon meringue pie. The cupcakes look great and taste even better.

TIP

Using readymade lemon curd cuts down the preparation time by around 15 minutes.

For the cupcakes
1 cup (2 sticks) sweet butter, softened
1 cup superfine sugar
2 cups sifted all-purpose flour
4 tsp. baking powder
5 large eggs
1 tsp. vanilla extract

For the lemon curd
1 cup granulated sugar
¼ cup cornstarch
⅛ tsp. salt
1¼ cups warm water
¼ cup fresh lemon juice
zest from 1 lemon
3 large egg yolks, lightly beaten
1 tbsp. unsalted butter

For the meringue
3 egg whites
¼ tsp. cream of tartar
⅓ cup granulated sugar

Preheat the oven to 350°F (175°C). Place 18 paper baking cups in muffin pans.

Place all the cupcake ingredients in a large bowl, and beat with an electric mixer until smooth and pale, about 2–3 minutes. Spoon the batter into the cups. Bake for 20 minutes. Remove pans from the oven and cool for 5 minutes. Then remove the cupcakes and cool on a rack.

For the lemon curd filling, combine the granulated sugar, cornstarch, and salt in a double boiler. Over low heat, slowly whisk in the warm water. Then add the lemon juice and zest, egg yolks, and butter. Cook, whisking constantly, until the mixture comes to a boil and thickens. The lemon curd should mound when dropped from a spoon. Remove from the heat. Press a sheet of parchment paper onto the surface to prevent a skin from forming, and cool thoroughly. Remove the top from each cupcake and hollow out a small hole. Spoon a little curd into the hole and replace the top.

For the meringue, beat the eggs and cream of tartar until soft peaks form. Add one-third of the sugar and beat for 1 minute. Repeat until all the sugar has been added. Increase the oven temperature to 450°F (230°C). Spoon or pipe the meringue on top of the cupcakes. Bake for 5 minutes until golden. Store for no more than 1 day in an airtight container.

Makes 1½ **dozen**

White Chocolate Devilish Cupcakes

These cupcakes are incredibly rich and moist delights!

For the cupcakes
2 cups sifted all-purpose flour
3 tsp. baking powder
1 cup packed light brown sugar
1 cup (2 sticks) sweet butter,
    softened
2 separated large eggs
3½ oz semisweet chocolate,
    melted
1 tsp. vanilla extract
½ cup milk

For the frosting
½ cup (1 stick) sweet butter,
    softened
1 tbsp. milk
3½ oz white chocolate, melted
1 tsp. vanilla extract
¾ cup confectioners' sugar, sifted

TIP

This recipe works equally well with the same amount of good quality white chocolate in place of the semisweet chocolate.

Preheat the oven to 350°F (175°C). Place 12 paper baking cups in a muffin pan.

Sift the flour and baking powder and set aside. In a medium bowl, cream the sugar and butter. Add the egg yolks and beat well. Add the melted chocolate and vanilla, mixing well. Add the flour and milk alternately, beating well with each addition. Beat the egg whites in a medium bowl until soft peaks form, and gently fold them into the batter.

Spoon the batter into the cups. Bake for 20 minutes. Remove pans from the oven and cool for 5 minutes. Then remove the cupcakes and cool on a rack. To make the frosting, cream the butter in a medium bowl. Beat in the milk until smooth. Stir in the chocolate and vanilla. Beat in the confectioners' sugar until thick and creamy. Spread over the cupcakes.

Store unfrosted in an airtight container for up to 2 days, or freeze for up to 3 months.

Makes 1 dozen

Choconana Cupcakes

The subtle flavor of banana perfectly complements the cream cheese frosting.

For the cupcakes
1 cup (2 sticks) sweet butter, softened
1 cup superfine sugar
2 cups sifted all-purpose flour
3 tsp. baking powder
5 large eggs
¼ tsp. nutmeg
1 cup (about 2 large) mashed ripe bananas
½ cup (3½ oz) semisweet chocolate chips

For the frosting
1 cup cream cheese
1½ cups confectioners' sugar, sifted
1 tbsp. lemon juice
1 tsp. vanilla extract
1 banana, thinly sliced

TIP
Walnut and cinnamon flavors work well with this cupcake.
You could try adding 3 tablespoons chopped walnuts and 1 teaspoon cinnamon to the frosting after creaming it.

Preheat the oven to 350˚F (175˚C). Place 18 paper baking cups in muffin pans.

Combine the butter, sugar, flour, eggs, and nutmeg in a large bowl and beat with an electric mixer until smooth, about 2–3 minutes. Stir in the mashed bananas and chocolate chips until well combined. Spoon the batter into the cups. Bake for 20 minutes. Remove pans from the oven and cool for 5 minutes. Then remove the cupcakes and cool on a rack.

To make the frosting, slowly beat the cream cheese in a large bowl with an electric mixer until it is soft and smooth. Add the confectioners' sugar, lemon juice, and vanilla. Beat briskly until smooth and well combined. Swirl the frosting onto the cooled cupcakes. Decorate each cupcake with a banana slice.

Store unfrosted in an airtight container for up to 2 days, or freeze for up to 3 months.

Makes 1½ dozen

Fudge-frosted Raisin Cupcakes

This fudge frosting is destined to bring even the mildest chocaholics to their knees!

For the cupcakes
1 cup (2 sticks) sweet butter, softened
1 cup superfine sugar
2 cups sifted all-purpose flour
3 tsp. baking powder
5 large eggs
1 tsp. vanilla extract
½ cup golden raisins

For the frosting
3½ oz semisweet chocolate, roughly chopped
2 tbsp. milk
¼ cup (½ stick) sweet butter
¾ cup confectioners' sugar, sifted

Preheat the oven to 350°F (175°C). Place 12 paper baking cups in a muffin pan.

Combine all the cupcake ingredients in a medium bowl and beat with an electric mixer until smooth and pale, about 2–3 minutes. Spoon the batter into the cups. Bake for 20 minutes. Remove the pans from the oven and cool for 5 minutes. Remove the cupcakes and cool on the rack.

To make the frosting, gently heat the chocolate, milk, and butter in a small, heavy saucepan, stirring until melted. Remove from the heat and beat in the confectioners' sugar. Swirl the frosting onto the cooled cupcakes.

Store unfrosted in an airtight container for up to 3 days, or freeze for up to 3 months.

Makes 1 dozen

Choco–orange Cupcakes

Chocolate and orange is always a winning combination.

For the cupcakes
½ cup (1 stick) sweet butter,
 softened
1 cup sugar
1 tsp. vanilla extract
2 extra-large eggs, separated and
 whites beaten until stiff
1¾ cup all-purpose flour
½ tsp. salt
2½ tsp. baking powder
½ cup orange juice

For the frosting
3½ oz semisweet chocolate,
 roughly chopped
2 tbsp. milk
¼ cup (½ stick) sweet butter
¾ cup confectioners' sugar, sifted
1 tsp. orange extract

TIP

Try replacing the orange juice with the same amount of cranberry juice drink, and replacing the orange extract in the frosting with 1 teaspoon dried cranberries.

Preheat the oven to 350°F (175°C). Place 18 paper baking cups in muffin pans.

Beat together the butter, sugar, and vanilla with an electric mixer until pale and fluffy. Gradually beat in the egg yolks. In a separate bowl, sift together the flour, salt, and baking powder. Add the dry ingredients to the creamed mixture a little at a time, alternating with a little of the orange juice until all mixed in. Fold in beaten egg whites.

Spoon the batter into the cups to come halfway up the sides. Bake for 10–15 minutes. Remove the pans from the oven and cool for 5 minutes. Remove the cupcakes and cool on the rack.

To make the frosting, gently heat the chocolate, milk, and butter in a small, heavy saucepan, stirring until melted. Remove from the heat and beat in the confectioners' sugar followed by the orange extract. Allow to cool, then swirl over the cupcakes with a small palate knife or spoon.

Store unfrosted in an airtight container for up to 3 days, or freeze for up to 3 months.

Makes 1½ dozen

Banana & Honey Cupcakes

Bananas lend themselves to natural sweeteners like maple syrup and honey.

1¾ cups (about 4 medium)
   mashed bananas
¾ cup packed light brown sugar
¼ cup honey
4 tbsp. margarine/butter, melted
2½ cups all-purpose flour
1 tsp. baking powder
pinch of salt
1 banana, sliced and chopped,
   to decorate

TIP

Add ¾ cup chopped walnuts to the batter to offset the sweetness and to give the cupcakes a little crunch.

Preheat the oven to 350°F (175°C). Place 18 paper baking cups in muffin pans.

In a bowl, combine the bananas, sugar, honey, and margarine. Beat with an electric mixer until well blended. Slowly add the flour, baking powder, and salt, and mix well. Spoon the batter into the cups, and top each cake with a slice of fresh banana. Bake for 20 minutes. Remove pans from the oven and cool for 5 minutes. Remove the cupcakes and cool on a rack.

Store in an airtight container for up to 2 days, or freeze for up to 3 months.

Makes 1½ dozen

Blueberry Cupcakes

These blueberry delights are spiced with nutmeg for a really wholesome buttery batch.

2 cups all-purpose flour
2½ tsp. baking powder
½ tsp. salt
¼ tsp. freshly grated nutmeg
¾ cup sugar
2 extra-large eggs
¾ cup milk
½ cup (1 stick) sweet butter, melted and cooled

shredded rind of half an orange
1 tsp. vanilla extract
½ cup fresh blueberries, mashed
2 cups fresh blueberries, plus extra to decorate
¼ cup powdered sugar, mixed with ¼ tsp. freshly grated nutmeg, for sprinkling

TIP

Decorate with three blueberries per cupcake, for a really pretty effect.

Preheat the oven to 325˚F (160˚C). Place 12 paper baking cups in a muffin pan.

Sift flour, baking powder, salt, and nutmeg into a large bowl. Stir in sugar, and make a well in the center.

In another bowl, beat eggs, milk, melted butter, orange rind, and vanilla extract, then stir in the mashed blueberries. Pour this mixture into the well, and lightly stir, until blended in. Do not overmix. Lightly fold in fresh blueberries.

Spoon batter into prepared cups, filling each three-quarters full. Sprinkle each with the sugar–nutmeg mixture, and bake until well risen and golden, for 25–30 minutes. Remove pan to a wire rack and let cool for about 2 minutes, then remove cupcakes to the wire rack to cool. Serve just warm or at room temperature.

Store in an airtight container for up to 3 days, or freeze in an airtight container for up to 3 months.

Makes 1 dozen

Frosted Flower Cupcakes

Cooking with flowers goes back centuries. You can find old recipes for flower water, jellies, conserves, and yes, cupcakes!

TIP

Tasty edible flowers that you could use for the decoration of these cupcakes include roses, mallows, pansies, nasturtiums, borage, marigolds, or chrysanthemums.

For the cupcakes
1 cup (2 sticks) sweet butter, softened
1 cup superfine sugar
2 cups all-purpose flour
2 tsp. baking powder
4 large eggs
1 tsp. vanilla extract

For the frosting
1¾ cups confectioners' sugar
2 tbsp. lemon juice
18 edible flower heads, stems removed
1 large egg white, very lightly whisked until just frothy

Preheat the oven to 350°F (175°C). Place 18 paper baking cups in muffin pans.

Combine all the cupcake ingredients in a large bowl and beat with an electric mixer until smooth and pale, about 2–3 minutes. Spoon the batter into the cups. Bake for 20 minutes. Remove pans from the oven and cool for 5 minutes. Then remove the cupcakes and cool on a rack.

To make the frosting, sift the confectioners' sugar into a medium bowl. Slowly add the lemon juice, stirring until the frosting holds its shape. Spread the frosting onto the cooled cupcakes.

To prepare the frosted flowers, put the egg white in a small bowl and some granulated sugar in another small bowl. Brush the petals with egg white on both sides. Dust with the sugar, place on a tray, and leave in a cool dry place to dry and stiffen. Lay on top of the frosted cupcakes.

Store in an airtight container for up to 3 days, or freeze unfrosted in an airtight container for up to 3 months.

Makes 1½ **dozen**

Poppy Seed Cupcakes with Lemon

The poppy seeds give these cupcakes a wonderful crunch!

For the cupcakes
1 cup (2 sticks) sweet butter, softened
1 cup superfine sugar
2 cups all-purpose flour
2½ tsp. baking powder
4 large eggs
1 tsp. vanilla extract
1 tbsp. poppy seeds
1 tbsp. grated lemon zest

For the drizzle
1 cup confectioners' sugar
4 tbsp. lemon juice
2 tbsp. poppy seeds

TIP

You could try replacing the lemon juice with lime or orange juice.

Preheat the oven to 350°F (175°C). Place 18 paper baking cups in muffin pans.

Combine the butter, sugar, flour, and eggs in a large bowl and beat with an electric mixer until smooth, about 2–3 minutes. Stir in the vanilla, poppy seeds, and lemon zest until well combined. Spoon the batter into the cups. Bake for 20 minutes. Remove pans from the oven and cool for 5 minutes. Then remove the cupcakes and cool on a rack.

To make the drizzle, sift the confectioners' sugar into a bowl and stir in the lemon juice until it resembles the consistency of heavy cream. Stir in the poppy seeds and drizzle over the cupcakes.

Store without frosting in an airtight container for up to 2 days, or freeze for up to 3 months.

Makes 1½ dozen

Lavender & Honey Cupcakes

The marriage of lavender and honey is truly wonderful. If you can find lavender honey, it will enhance the flavor even more.

For the cupcakes
1 cup (2 sticks) sweet butter, softened
1 cup superfine sugar
2 cups all-purpose flour
2½ tsp. baking powder
4 large eggs
1 tsp. vanilla extract

For the frosting
1½ cups confectioners' sugar, sifted
⅓ cup honey
1 tsp. lemon juice
2 tbsp. dried lavender flowers, stalks removed
1 tsp. lemon zest

TIP

Try stirring a drop of blue food coloring into the frosting to get a striking blue topping that complements the lavender flowers beautifully.

Preheat the oven to 400˚F (200˚C). Place 18 baking cups in muffin pans.

Combine all the cupcake ingredients in a medium bowl and beat with an electric mixer until smooth and pale, about 2–3 minutes. Spoon the batter into the cups. Bake for 20 minutes. Remove pans from the oven and cool for 5 minutes. Then remove the cupcakes and cool on a rack.

For the frosting, beat the confectioners' sugar with the honey and lemon juice. Stir in half of the lavender flowers. Spread the frosting onto the cupcakes and sprinkle with the reserved lavender flowers and lemon zest.

Store without frosting in an airtight container for up to 3 days, or freeze for up to 3 months.

Makes 1½ dozen

Strawberry Cupcakes

Chocolate baskets filled with Kirsch cream and fresh strawberries are delightful treats to serve at a dinner party.

For the cupcakes
8 oz. semisweet chocolate
½ cup sweet butter
4 tbsp. light corn syrup
5½ cups cornflakes

For the frosting
1¼ cups heavy cream
1 tbsp. confectioners' sugar
2 tbsp. kirsch or brandy
2 cups fresh strawberries, hulled
  and finely chopped
12 fresh strawberries,
  to decorate

TIP

You could replace the strawberries and kirsch with a variety of different fruits. Soak ½ cup large raisins in 4 tablespoons dark rum and place inside the chocolate cups.

Place the chocolate, butter, and syrup in a double boiler. Allow the chocolate to melt completely before stirring. Put the cornflakes in a plastic food bag and crush lightly with a rolling pin. Add the cornflakes to the melted chocolate and stir to coat evenly.

Divide the chocolate mixture between 12 cups in a nonstick muffin pan. Using a teaspoon, press the mixture into the base and up the side of each cup. Chill in the refrigerator.

Combine the cream and confectioners' sugar in a bowl and beat until smooth. Fold in the liqueur. Remove the muffin pan from the refrigerator. Using a palette knife carefully remove the chocolate cups from the pan. Divide the chopped strawberries between the cups. Fill each with a dollop or swirl of cream and top with a fresh strawberry. Chill until required.

Serve decorated with fresh mint leaves, if desired.

Makes 1 dozen

Black Forest Cupcakes

Sweet juicy berries and creamy white chocolate go together so well. These delicious light and fluffy cupcakes are perfect served with afternoon tea.

For the cupcakes
3 extra-large eggs
¾ cup superfine sugar
1½ cups all-purpose flour
1½ tsp. baking powder
¾ cup (1½ sticks) sweet butter
4 oz frozen cherries and
   blackberries, pitted
⅔ cup white chocolate chips

For the frosting
1¼ cups whipping cream
2 tbsp. confectioners' sugar
1 tsp. vanilla extract
24–48 fresh raspberries,
   to decorate
fresh mint leaves, to decorate

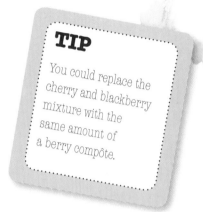

TIP

You could replace the cherry and blackberry mixture with the same amount of a berry compôte.

Preheat the oven to 350°F (175°C). Line two 12-cup muffin pans with paper baking cups. Thaw the black forest fruit mixture, reserving the juice.

Combine the eggs, sugar, flour, and butter in a large bowl. Beat for 3–4 minutes with an electric mixer until the mixture is pale and smooth. Gently fold in the thawed fruit mixture with the juice and chocolate chips. Divide the mixture between the paper baking cups and bake for 15 minutes until well risen and golden brown. Remove from the oven and cool for 5 minutes. Transfer to a wire rack to cool completely.

Beat the cream, confectioners' sugar, and vanilla with an electric mixer until soft peaks form. Swirl the frosting over the cupcakes and decorate with a raspberry and mint leaves. Store unfrosted in an airtight container for up to 3 days. Use frosted cakes on the day they are decorated.

Makes 2 dozen

Coffee & Walnut Cupcakes

Coffee and walnuts are a sublime pairing in this golden, crumbly cake with its rich coffee butter frosting. A favorite for generations and an absolute must on any tea table.

For the cupcakes
¾ cup (1½ sticks) butter, at room temperature
generous ¾ cup superfine sugar
3 extra-large eggs
1¼ cups all-purpose flour
½ tsp. baking powder
½ cup walnut pieces
2½ tsp. instant coffee, dissolved in 1 tbsp. hot water

For the frosting
2 tbsp. milk
2 tsp. instant coffee
¾ stick butter, at room temperature
1¼ cups confectioners' sugar, sifted
walnut halves, to decorate

TIP

Brazil nuts, pecans, macadamia nuts, or hazelnuts could also work well with this coffee-flavored recipe.

Preheat the oven to 350°F (175°C). Line two 12-cup muffin pans with paper baking cups.

Beat the butter and sugar together until pale and creamy, then beat in the eggs one at a time. Sift the flour over the butter mixture and stir in. Fold in the walnuts and coffee. Divide the mixture between the paper baking cups and spread out evenly. Bake for 15 minutes until golden and the cupcakes spring back when pressed gently. Transfer to a wire rack to cool.

To make the frosting, warm the milk and coffee in a pan, stirring until the coffee has dissolved. Pour into a bowl, leaving to cool until just warm before adding the butter and confectioners' sugar. Beat together until smooth and creamy. Spread the frosting over the cooled cupcakes then decorate with walnut halves.

Store unfrosted in an airtight container for up to 3 days. Use frosted cakes on the day they are decorated.

Makes 2 dozen

Apple & Cinnamon Cupcakes

This simple cupcake layered with tangy apples makes a good choice as a no-fuss treat to serve with coffee.

½ cup (1 stick) sweet butter, at
　　room temperature
¾ cup light brown sugar
¼ cup sour cream
1½ tsp. ground cinnamon
2 extra-large eggs

1½ cups all-purpose flour
½ tsp. baking powder
1½ apples, peeled, cored,
　　and sliced
4 tbsp. apricot jelly

TIP

To transform these into desserts, try serving with a dollop or two of sour cream and some fresh blueberries.

Preheat the oven to 350°F (175°C). Line two 12-cup muffin pans with paper baking cups.

Beat together the butter and sugar until smooth and creamy, then beat in the sour cream and cinnamon. Beat in the eggs one at a time, then sift the flour over the top and fold in.

Spoon about half the batter into the paper baking cups, then top with a layer of apple slices. Spoon on the remaining batter, and top with another layer of apples, arranging the slices neatly. Bake for about 20 minutes until risen and golden and a skewer inserted in the center comes out clean. Let cool in the pans for a few minutes, then turn out on a wire rack to cool.

While the cupcakes are still warm, heat the apricot jelly in a small saucepan until it is warm, then brush over the top of the cakes to glaze.

Store in an airtight container for up to 2 days, or freeze for up to 3 months.

Makes 2 dozen

Everyday Cupcakes

Cupcakes are the perfect size for everyday additions to lunch, with afternoon tea, or when you are on the go. These recipes are simple and quick, with flavors you'll crave on a regular basis.

Everyday Cupcakes

A cupcake a day keeps the hunger at bay! Whether you need to add a little "oomph" to your breakfast or keep a supply of tasty snacks, these recipes are the easiest to make. If you're going to bake big batches and slowly work your way through them, there are some handy hints and tips to keep your cupcakes fresh, light, and fluffy for as long as a week after they come out of the oven.

The cocoa in Cappuccino Cupcakes will dry them out faster than vanilla-based recipes. Store in an airtight container as soon as possible. If they're going to be out on display, frost the top of the cake right to the edges of the case, and this helps seal in moisture. The same rule applies to all cupcake recipes that call for cocoa. For even longer shelf life, warm a spoonful of apricot jelly and brush lightly over the cake top before frosting.

The recipes that will keep the longest contain either fresh fruit, such as banana, or maple syrup, both of which hold in moisture. Frosting any cupcake to the edge of the case will prolong its life, and you can even put a thin layer of marzipan over the top beforehand. Your everyday cupcakes will be delicious morning, noon, and night.

Cappuccino Cupcakes

This unusual frosting only takes a couple of minutes to make. Once these cupcakes are frosted you can let them set or eat while they're still sticky—it's up to you!

For the cupcakes
3 extra-large eggs
¾ cup superfine sugar
1½ cups all-purpose flour
½ tsp. baking powder
¼ cup Dutch-process cocoa powder
¾ cup (1½ sticks) sweet butter
½ cup semisweet chocolate chips
1 tbsp. milk

For the frosting
4 oz white chocolate chips
2½ tbsp. cold black strong coffee
1 cup confectioners' sugar, sifted
3 tbsp. chocolate sprinkles

Preheat the oven to 350°F (175°C). Line two 12-cup muffin pans with paper baking cups.

Combine all the cupcake ingredients in a large bowl and beat for 3–4 minutes with an electric mixer until smooth. Divide the mixture between the cups and bake for 15 minutes until well risen and golden brown. Remove from the oven and cool for 5 minutes. Transfer to a wire rack to cool completely.

Put the white chocolate chips and coffee in a double boiler and heat until melted. Remove from the heat and stir in the confectioners' sugar. Spread the frosting over the cupcakes and sprinkle with the chocolate sprinkles. Store in an airtight container for up to 4 days.

Makes 2 dozen

Peach Granola Cupcakes

If you are usually in a hurry to get out the door in the morning, make a batch of these delicious and nutritious muffins the night before.

1 cup (7 oz) finely chopped dried peaches
1¼ cups dried granola
2¼ cups all-purpose flour
1½ tsp. baking powder
½ cup orange juice
½ cup apple juice
3 tbsp. vegetable oil
¾ cup honey
1 large lightly beaten egg

Preheat the oven to 350˚F (175˚C). Place 12 paper baking cups in a muffin pan.

Mix the peaches, granola, flour, and baking powder in a medium bowl with a spoon. Set aside. Beat the orange juice, apple juice, oil, honey, and egg in a large bowl with an electric mixer. Add the flour mixture to the egg mixture, and stir until just combined.

Spoon the mixture into the prepared pan. Bake for 20 minutes. Remove pan from the oven and cool for 5 minutes. Then remove from the pan and cool on a rack.

Store in an airtight container for up to 3 days, or freeze for up to 3 months.

Makes 1 dozen

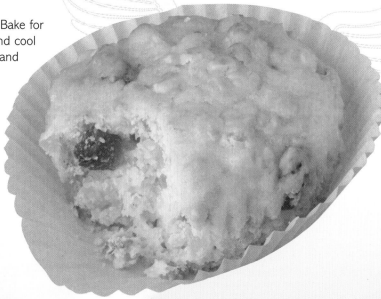

Cardamom & Orange Cupcakes

Cardamom has a unique taste and is highly aromatic. Though it is a staple component of Indian curries, it is often also used in baking, and smells simply delicious!

For the cupcakes
1 cup (2 sticks) sweet butter, softened
1 cup superfine sugar
2 cups all-purpose flour
1 tsp. baking powder
5 large eggs
1 tsp. ground cardamom
1 tsp. orange extract

For the frosting
2 cups confectioners' sugar, sifted
½ cup (1 stick) sweet butter, softened
¼ cup sour cream
1½ tbsp. grated orange zest
1 tsp. orange extract
36 cardamom pods, to decorate

Preheat the oven to 350°F (175°C). Place 18 paper baking cups in muffin pans.

Combine all the cupcake ingredients in a medium bowl and beat with an electric mixer until smooth and pale, about 2–3 minutes.

Spoon the batter into the cups. Bake in the oven for 20 minutes. Remove pans from the oven and cool for 5 minutes. Then remove the cupcakes and cool on a rack.

To make the frosting, beat the confectioners' sugar, butter, sour cream, orange zest, and orange extract with an electric mixer until smooth. Spread the frosting on the cupcakes and top each with 2 cardamom pods. Store unfrosted for up to 2 days in an airtight container, or freeze for up to 3 months.

Makes 1½ dozen

Fig & Vanilla Cupcakes

Dried figs are sweeter than fresh figs. Indeed, the Ancient Romans used dried figs as sweeteners because cane sugar was so rare and expensive.

For the cupcakes
1 cup (2 sticks) sweet butter, softened
1 cup superfine sugar
2 cups all-purpose flour
2 tsp. baking powder
5 large eggs
1 tbsp. vanilla extract
1 cup (5 oz) finely chopped, dried figs

For the frosting
1 cup cream cheese, softened
1½ cups confectioners' sugar, sifted
⅓ cup honey
1 tsp. vanilla extract
1 tbsp. grated lemon zest
3 tbsp. chopped figs

TIP

Try adding 1 teaspoon ground ginger and ¼ cup candied sugar after combining the cream cheese and confectioner's sugar.

Preheat the oven to 350°F (175°C). Place 18 baking cups in muffin pans.

Combine all the cupcake ingredients in a large bowl and beat with an electric mixer until smooth and pale, about 2–3 minutes. Spoon the batter into the cups. Bake for 20 minutes. Remove pans from the oven and cool for 5 minutes. Then remove the cupcakes and cool on a rack.

To make the frosting, beat the cream cheese, confectioners' sugar, honey, vanilla, and lemon zest with an electric mixer until soft and creamy. Smear the cupcakes with the frosting. Store unfrosted in an airtight container for up to 2 days, or freeze for up to 3 months.

Makes 1½ **dozen**

Rosewater & Pomegranate Cupcakes

Rosewater is a delicate, sweet flavoring made by steeping rose petals in water, oil, or alcohol.

For the cupcakes
1 cup (2 sticks) sweet butter, softened
1 cup superfine sugar
2 cups all-purpose flour
1 tsp. baking powder
5 large eggs
1 tsp. rosewater

For the frosting
1 cup cream cheese
1½ cups confectioners' sugar, sifted
3 tbsp. pomegranate seeds
2 tbsp. rosewater
3 tbsp. pistachios, chopped

TIP
Try to use sweet rather than salted pistachios for this recipe.

Preheat the oven to 350˚F (175˚C). Place 18 paper baking cups in muffin pans.

Combine all the cupcake ingredients in a medium bowl and beat with an electric mixer until smooth and pale, about 2–3 minutes.

Spoon the batter into the cups. Bake for 20 minutes. Remove pans from the oven and cool for 5 minutes. Then remove the cupcakes and cool on a rack.

For the frosting, combine the cream cheese and confectioners' sugar, and beat with an electric mixer until soft and creamy. Add the pomegranate seeds, rosewater, and pistachios, and stir well. Swirl onto the top of the cupcakes.

Store without frosting for up to 3 days in an airtight container, or freeze for up to 3 months.

Makes 1½ dozen

White Chocolate and Chili Cupcakes

This is a delicious combination of chocolate and tingling chili.

For the cupcakes
1 cup (2 sticks) sweet butter,
  softened
1 cup superfine sugar
1½ cups all-purpose flour
4 tbsp. Dutch-process cocoa powder
2 tsp. baking powder
4 large eggs
2 tsp. chipotle chili powder
½ cup (3½ oz) white
  chocolate chips

For the frosting
1½ cups confectioners' sugar, sifted
½ cup Dutch-process cocoa powder
3 tbsp. Tia Maria
½ cup (1 stick) sweet butter,
  softened

TIP

For even more of a chili kick, you could add 1 teaspoon chili flakes to the frosting.

Preheat the oven to 350°F (175°C). Place 18 paper baking cups in muffin pans. Combine all the cupcake ingredients, except the chocolate chips, in a large bowl and beat with an electric mixer until smooth, about 2–3 minutes. Stir in the chocolate chips.

Spoon the batter into the cups. Bake for 20 minutes. Remove pans from the oven and cool for 5 minutes. Then remove the cupcakes and cool on a rack.

To make the frosting, blend all the ingredients together in a food processor. Spread the frosting on the cooled cupcakes. Store unfrosted in an airtight container for up to 2 days, or freeze for up to 3 months.

Makes 1½ dozen

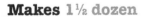

Crème de Menthe Cupcakes

Mint is a versatile herb that complements both sweet and savory dishes and goes especially well with chocolate.

For the cupcakes
1½ cups all-purpose flour
4 tbsp. Dutch-process cocoa powder
1½ tsp. baking powder
1 cup superfine sugar
1 cup (2 sticks) sweet butter,
  softened
4 large eggs
1 tsp. mint extract
½ cup (3½ oz) mint chocolate chips

For the frosting
⅓ cup (⅔ stick) sweet butter,
  softened
2 cups confectioners' sugar, sifted
1 tbsp. crème de menthe
green food coloring
½ cup (3½ oz) chocolate flakes,
  chopped into 3-in. lengths
chocolate syrup, to drizzle

TIP

You could try adding ½ cup golden raisins along with the chocolate chips in the cupcake mix.

Preheat the oven to 325°F (160°C). Place 18 paper baking cups in muffin pans.

In a medium bowl, sift together the flour, cocoa, and baking powder. Set aside. Beat the sugar and butter together in a large bowl until smooth. Add the eggs one at a time, beating well after each addition. Add the flour mixture gradually, stirring until well combined. Stir in the mint extract and chocolate chips. Spoon the mixture into the cups. Bake for 20 minutes. Remove the pans from the oven and cool for 5 minutes. Then remove the cupcakes and cool on a rack.

To make the frosting, beat the butter and confectioners' sugar in a small bowl until smooth and creamy. Stir in the crème de menthe and just enough food coloring to turn the frosting a mint green. Frost the cupcakes and decorate with a chocolate flake and a drizzle of chocolate syrup. Store unfrosted in an airtight container for up to 3 days, or freeze for up to 3 months.

Makes 1½ **dozen**

Chocolate, Orange & Prune Cupcakes

The combination of bittersweet chocolate and prunes makes this cupcake pure decadence.

For the cupcakes
1 cup (2 sticks) sweet butter, softened
1 cup superfine sugar
2 cups all-purpose flour
1½ tsp. baking powder
5 large eggs
1 tsp. vanilla extract

1 tbsp. finely grated orange zest
½ cup (3½ oz) bittersweet chocolate chips
½ cup (3½ oz) chopped dried prunes

For the frosting
1½ cups confectioners' sugar, sifted
½ cup (1 stick) sweet butter, softened
¾ cup Dutch-process cocoa powder
2 tbsp. chocolate liqueur
1 tsp. vanilla extract

TIP

You could try soaking the prunes in warm water for an hour or so first—they will absorb the flavors more easily.

Preheat the oven to 350°F (175°C). Place 18 paper baking cups in muffin pans.

Combine all the cupcake ingredients, except the chocolate chips and prunes, in a large bowl and beat with an electric mixer until smooth and pale, about 2–3 minutes. Stir in the prunes and chocolate. Spoon the batter into the cups. Bake in the oven for 20 minutes. Remove pans from the oven and cool for 5 minutes. Then remove the cupcakes and cool on a rack.

For the frosting, beat the confectioners' sugar and butter in a small bowl until creamy and smooth. Beat in the cocoa. Fold in the chocolate liqueur and vanilla. Spread the frosting onto the cooled cupcakes.

Store in an airtight container for up to 3 days, or freeze, unfrosted, for up to 3 months.

Makes 1½ dozen

Coconut and Chocolate Cupcakes

Toasted coconut and creamy white chocolate—a sensational combination that will keep you coming back for more!

For the cupcakes
5 large eggs
⅔ cup superfine sugar
1 cup all-purpose flour
1 tsp. baking powder
1 cup dry unsweetened
   flaked coconut
½ cup (1 stick) sweet butter, melted

For the frosting
4 oz white chocolate chunks
2 tbsp. toasted flaked coconut

TIP

You could try half filling the paper cups, adding a raspberry, and then spooning the rest of the mixture in for a raspberry surprise in the center.

Preheat the oven to 400°F (200°C). Line two 12-cup muffin pans with paper baking cups.

Combine the eggs and sugar in a large bowl and beat with an electric mixer for 2–3 minutes, until smooth. Sift the flour and baking powder over the top of the creamed mixture. Using a metal spoon, lightly fold in the flour, and baking powder using a figure of 8 movement. Add the coconut and melted butter and continue to fold in gently. Divide the mixture between the cups. Bake for 10 minutes, or until well risen and golden brown. Remove from the oven and cool for 5 minutes. Transfer to a wire rack to cool completely.

To make the frosting, melt the chocolate in a double boiler, and stir until smooth. Using a fork, drizzle a little melted chocolate over the top of each cupcake and sprinkle with coconut. Allow the chocolate to cool completely before serving.

Store in an airtight container for up to 4 days, or freeze, unfrosted, for up to 3 months.

Makes 1 dozen

Madeira Cupcakes

Sometimes the simplest cupcakes are the best, and these simple, golden, lemony cakes are no exception.

1 cup (2 sticks) sweet butter, at room temperature
generous ¾ cup superfine sugar, plus 1–2 tbsp. for sprinkling
3 extra-large eggs
1¾ cups all-purpose flour

2 tsp. baking powder
finely grated zest and juice of 1 lemon
1–2 tbsp. sugar

TIP

Madeira cake was traditionally served with a glass of Madeira wine in the nineteenth century (hence its name) but these cupcakes are just as delicious with a cup of tea or coffee.

Preheat the oven to 350°F (175°C). Place 18 paper baking cups in muffin pans.

Beat together the butter and sugar until pale and creamy, then beat in the eggs one at a time. Sift the flour and baking powder over the mixture, then fold it in. Fold in the lemon zest and juice.

Divide the mixture between the cups. Sprinkle the top with sugar and bake for 15–20 minutes or until well risen and golden brown. Turn them out onto wire racks to cool.

Remove the pans from the oven and cool for 5 minutes. Then remove the cupcakes and cool on a rack.

Makes 18

Dundee Cupcakes

This citrusy version of the English fruit cake improves with keeping, so if you can, make these a couple of days in advance and store in an airtight container until ready to serve.

¾ cup (1½ sticks) butter
½ cup superfine sugar
generous ¼ cup light brown sugar
3 extra-large eggs
finely grated zest of 1 orange
1⅓ cups all-purpose flour
1½ tsp. baking powder

2 tbsp. brandy
1⅓ cups mixed dried vine fruits
(raisins, golden raisins, currants)
¼ cup candied cherries, halved
⅓ cup blanched almonds,
   to decorate

TIP

If you prefer, you could omit the orange zest and add 2 teaspoons instant coffee dissolved in 1 tablespoon water.

Preheat the oven to 350°F (175°C). Place 18 paper baking cups in muffin pans.

Cream the butter and sugars together until fluffy, then beat in the eggs one at a time. Stir in the orange zest, then sift the flour and baking powder over the top and stir in. Mix in the brandy followed by the dried vine fruits and candied cherries.

Tip the mixture into the prepared cups, then scatter the almonds on top. Bake for 15–20 minutes until dark golden and well risen.

Cool in the pans for 5 minutes, then turn out onto a wire rack to cool completely. Store in an airtight container for up to 3 days, or freeze for up to 3 months.

Makes 1½ **dozen**

Floral Cupcakes

Perfect for when your day needs brightening, these simple vanilla cupcakes have a glorious display of flowers.

TIP

Instead of bought sugar flowers, decorate with homemade frosted petals (see page 234).

For the cupcakes
¾ cup sugar
3½ fl. oz cream
1½ tbsp. butter
seeds from 1 vanilla bean
1¾ cups all-purpose flour
2 tsp. baking powder
3 tbsp. cornstarch
1 small banana

pinch of salt
3 extra-large eggs

For the frosting
scant 1 cup (7 fl. oz) heavy cream
approx. ⅓ cup confectioners' sugar,
   or to taste
24 sugar flowers, to decorate

Preheat the oven to 350°F (175°C). Place 12 paper baking cups in a muffin pan. Put ½ cup sugar, the cream, and butter into a pan and bring to the boil. Add the vanilla seeds and simmer over a low heat for 5 minutes, then let cool.

Mix the flour, baking powder, and cornstarch. Peel and purée the banana, and whisk into the vanilla cream with the rest of the sugar and the salt. Mix in the eggs. Then quickly mix in the dry ingredients.

Spoon the mixture into the paper cases. Bake in the oven for 20–30 minutes. Cool in the muffin pan for 5 minutes, then take out and cool on a cake rack.

To make the frosting, beat the cream with the confectioners' sugar until smooth. Pipe on top of the cupcakes and decorate with the sugar flowers.

Makes 1 dozen

Sticky Maple Pecan Cupcakes

These buttery cupcakes, with their fragrant flavor of maple syrup and pecans, are especially wonderful with a steaming hot cup of coffee. The bitterness of the coffee perfectly offsets the sugary sweetness of the cakes.

For the cupcakes
¾ cup (1½ sticks) sweet butter, at room temperature
¾ cup superfine sugar
3 extra-large eggs
scant 1¼ cups all-purpose flour
1¾ tsp. baking powder
½ cup pecans, roughly chopped

For the frosting
½ cup (1 stick) sweet butter, at room temperature
2 tbsp. pure maple syrup
1 tbsp. milk
1⅓ cups confectioners' sugar, sifted
pecan halves, to decorate

TIP
Walnuts or Brazil nuts could also work well in this recipe.

Preheat the oven to 350°F (175°C). Place 18 paper baking cups in muffin pans.

Beat the butter and sugar together until pale and creamy, then beat in the eggs one at a time. Sift the flour and baking powder over the egg mixture, then fold in. Add the pecans and fold in.

Tip the mixture into the prepared cups, and bake for 15–20 minutes until golden and well risen.

Let cool in the pan for about 20 minutes, then turn out onto a wire rack to cool completely.

To decorate, beat together the butter, syrup, milk, and confectioners' sugar until smooth and creamy. Spread over the cupcakes and top with the pecan halves.

Store unfrosted in an airtight container for up to 3 days, or freeze for up to 3 months.

Makes 1½ dozen

Fig & Date Cupcakes

These cakes are based on a traditional Polish recipe.

6 large eggs, separated
½ cup superfine sugar
1 tsp. vanilla extract
1 cup all-purpose flour
1 tsp. baking powder
½ cup raisins

⅓ cup chopped dried figs
⅓ cup cooking dates, chopped
3 tbsp. chopped mixed peel
confectioners' sugar to dredge

Preheat the oven to 400°F (200°C). Place 18 paper baking cups in muffin pans.

Beat the egg yolks and sugar in a bowl until pale and thick. Lightly stir in the vanilla, then fold in the flour and baking powder. Stir in all the fruit. Whisk the egg whites until stiff and stir a couple of spoonfuls into the mixture to lighten it, then fold in the remainder (this is not easy as the mixture is fairly stiff but try not to over-stir while mixing in the whites). Spoon the batter into the cups. Bake for 15–20 minutes or until risen, golden and firm to the touch. Cool on a wire rack. Decorate with confectioners' sugar before serving.

Store in an airtight container for up to 3 days, or freeze for up to 3 months.

Makes 1½ **dozen**

Gingerbread & Maple Syrup Cupcakes

These cupcakes are moist and satisfying, and the maple syrup cream frosting is simple but complements the ginger perfectly.

For the cupcakes
2 cups all-purpose flour
2 tsp. baking powder
1½ tsp. baking soda
½ tsp. salt
1 tsp. each ground cinnamon and
    ground ginger
½ tsp. freshly grated nutmeg
¼ tsp. ground cloves
⅛ tsp. freshly ground black pepper
½ cup (1 stick) sweet butter

¼ cup superfine sugar
½ cup dark molasses
¼ cup clear honey
1 extra-large egg, lightly beaten
1 tsp. vanilla extract
½ cup buttermilk

For the cream
2 tbsp. maple syrup
½ cup whipped heavy cream

TIP

If you prefer, you could add a little chopped stem ginger into the maple syrup cream and serve it on the side.

Preheat the oven to 350°F (175°C). Line two 12-cup muffin pans with paper baking cups. Sift flour, baking powder, baking soda, salt, cinnamon, ginger, nutmeg, cloves, and pepper into a bowl.

In a bowl with an electric mixer, beat butter and sugar together until light and fluffy, about 2 minutes. On low speed, beat in molasses and honey until well blended, scraping down side of bowl once. Then beat in egg and vanilla extract.

Lightly stir in the flour mixture and buttermilk alternately in batches until well blended. Divide the mixture between the cups. Bake for 15–20 minutes until well risen and golden brown. Transfer to a wire rack to cool, about 10 minutes, then remove from the pans. Stir the maple syrup into the cream, then spoon over the cupcakes.

Store unfrosted in an airtight container for up to 3 days, or freeze for up to 3 months.

Makes 2 dozen

Cupcakes for Kids

Easy and simple recipes that the kids will love
to both make and eat are to be found in this
chapter. They'll find it hard to resist the
candy-covered, sugar-crusted cupcakes
on offer—and so will you!

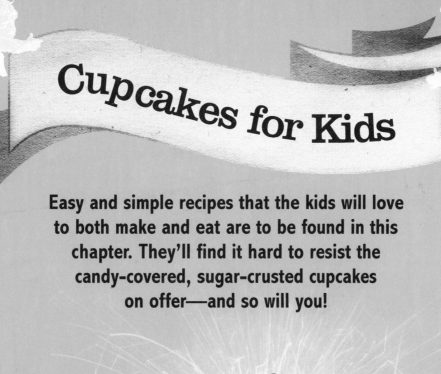

Cupcakes for Kids

Cupcakes always go down well with little kids and big kids. Children love sweet and sticky recipes, fun decorations, and frosting piped so high they can't take a bite without a nose-full of sugar. Unfortunately, these days throwing a kids' party means thinking about allergies, food intolerances, and general hyperactivity. Luckily, some of these recipes are very easy to adapt.

If you're dealing with gluten or dairy allergies, Spider's Web Cupcakes are made with very little flour. Replace with gluten-free and you'll hardly notice the difference. To deal with dairy, replace butter with a hard dairy-free margarine and frost with a little light cool whip. Similarly, nut allergies can pose problems for kids' parties. Do not try to make alternative batches, one with nuts and the other without. You can't risk any mix-ups.

If you're worried about sugar content, substitute frosting for light cool whip and decorate with sprinkles. The children will never know the difference. Many parents are also concerned about artificial colors and flavorings; if you want to serve up fun cupcakes without the E-numbers, decorate with chocolate chips or purchase all-natural food colors and sprinkles from your local baking store. Even with alterations, these cupcakes will never fail to impress the kids.

Spider's Web Cupcakes

Get scary at parties with these fabulously moist and succulent cupcakes made with roast squash or pumpkin. Look for toy spiders in toy stores to decorate them with (Just remember to warn your guests they're not edible—in case they get carried away!)

For the cupcakes
¾ lb peeled, seeded butternut squash or pumpkin, cut into chunks
½ tbsp. vegetable oil
½ cup (1 stick) sweet butter, at room temperature
¾ cup light brown sugar
3 extra-large eggs
½ tsp. ground ginger
1½ tsp. ground cinnamon
scant 1¼ cups all-purpose flour
1¾ tsp. baking powder

For the frosting
7 oz bittersweet chocolate, chopped
¾ cup whipping cream
1 oz white chocolate

TIP

Add ½ teaspoon crushed dried chili flakes into the mixture with the ginger and cinnamon for a real kick to the recipe.

Preheat oven to 375°F (190°C). Put squash in a baking dish, drizzle with the oil, and toss to coat. Roast for about 35 minutes until tender. Remove and let cool, then mash to a coarse purée. Reduce oven temperature to 350°F (175°C). Line two 12-cup muffin pans with paper baking cups.

Beat the butter and sugar together until smooth and creamy. Beat in the eggs one at a time, then stir in the ginger and cinnamon. Sift the flour and baking powder over the bowl and fold in, then fold in the mashed squash. Divide the mixture between the cups. Bake for 15–20 minutes until well risen and golden brown. Remove from the oven and cool for 5 minutes. Transfer to a wire rack to cool completely.

For the frosting, put the chopped bittersweet chocolate in a heatproof bowl. Heat the cream until almost boiling, then pour over the chocolate. Let stand for 5 minutes, then stir until smooth. Let cool and thicken slightly.

Melt the white chocolate in a heatproof bowl set over a pan of barely simmering water. Using a teaspoon, spoon the frosting over the cupcakes. Spoon the melted white chocolate into a piping bag, then pipe two small concentric circles on the cupcakes. Draw a skewer from the center to the outside to create a spider web effect. Store unfrosted in an airtight container for up to 3 days. Use frosted cakes on the day they are decorated.

Makes 2 dozen

Ice Cream Cupcakes

These cupcakes look like ice cream—but they won't melt!

For the cupcakes
1 cup (2 sticks) sweet butter,
  softened
1 cup superfine sugar
2 cups all-purpose flour
2 tsp. baking powder
4 large eggs
1 tsp. vanilla extract

For the frosting
1½ cups confectioners' sugar,
  sifted
¼ cup (½ stick) sweet butter,
  softened
pinch of salt
½ cup heavy cream
1 tsp. vanilla extract
2 tbsp. colored sprinkles

TIP

For a really striking kids' party cupcake, you could place the cooled cupcakes inside ice cream cones before you add the frosting.

Preheat the oven to 350°F (175°C). Line a 24-cup mini muffin pan with paper baking cups.

Combine all the cupcake ingredients in a large bowl and beat with an electric mixer until smooth and pale, about 2–3 minutes. Spoon the batter into the cups. Bake for 20 minutes. Remove pan from the oven and cool for 5 minutes. Then remove the cupcakes and cool on a rack.

To make the frosting, beat the confectioners' sugar, butter, and salt using an electric mixer. Add the cream and vanilla, and beat until smooth. Pipe the mixture in a swirl on top of the cupcake. Shake some sprinkles on top.

Store unfrosted in an airtight container for up to 3 days, or freeze for up to 3 months.

Makes 2 dozen

Butterfly Cupcakes with Jelly

Kids will love these delicate little cakes, which can be served for afternoon tea or as a dessert.

For the cupcakes
1 cup (2 sticks) sweet butter, softened
1 cup superfine sugar
2 cups all-purpose flour
2 tsp. baking powder
4 large eggs
1 tsp. vanilla extract

For the frosting
½ cup (1 stick) sweet butter
2 cups confectioners' sugar, sifted
1 tsp. vanilla extract
½ cup strawberry jelly, to decorate

TIP
Add 1 tablespoon lemon zest to the frosting for a flavorful addition.

Preheat the oven to 350˚F (175˚C). Place 18 paper baking cups in muffin pans. Combine all ingredients for the cupcakes in a large bowl and beat with an electric mixer until smooth and pale, about 2–3 minutes.

Spoon the batter into the cups. Bake for 20 minutes. Remove pans from the oven and cool for 5 minutes. Then remove the cupcakes and cool on a rack.

Prepare the frosting by beating the butter, confectioners' sugar, and vanilla until smooth. Cut a slice from the top of each cake and cut it into two. Pipe or spoon the frosting onto the flattened top of each cupcake. Then place the half-circles of cake at an angle on each side of the frosting. Decorate with a teaspoon of strawberry jelly, at the center of the butterfly wings.

Store unfrosted in an airtight container for up to 3 days, or freeze for up to 3 months.

Makes 1½ dozen

Vanilla Cupcakes with Choc Frosting

These fun cupcakes will brighten up any kid's party.

For the cupcakes
3 large eggs
¾ cup superfine sugar
1½ cups all-purpose flour
1¾ tsp. baking powder
¾ cups (1½ sticks) sweet butter
　(or margarine)
1 tsp. vanilla extract

For the frosting
1 cup (2 sticks) sweet butter,
　softened
1 cup confectioners' sugar, sifted
3 tbsp. Dutch-process
　cocoa powder
1 tbsp. milk
M&Ms to decorate

TIP

This vanilla cupcake recipe can easily be adapted to other simple recipes. Omit the vanilla extract and replace with 3 tablespoons orange marmalade before baking.

Preheat the oven to 350°F (175°C). Line two 12-cup muffin pans with paper baking cups.

Put all the cupcake ingredients in a large bowl and beat with an electric mixer for 3–4 minutes, until the mixture is smooth and pale. Divide the mixture between the cups. Bake for 15 minutes until well risen and golden brown. Remove from the oven and cool for 5 minutes. Transfer to a wire rack to cool completely.

For the frosting, combine the butter, confectioners' sugar, cocoa, and milk in a large bowl and beat until smooth. Spoon into a frosting bag fitted with a medium star nozzle and pipe a large swirl of frosting on top of each cupcake. Scatter each cupcake with 5 or 6 M&Ms.

Store unfrosted in an airtight container for up to 2 days.

Makes 2 dozen

Fairy Princess Cupcakes

These delicious squishy cakes will be demolished by the kids in no time.

For the cupcakes
⅓ cup margarine or sweet butter
1 cups dark brown sugar, packed
2 extra-large eggs, beaten
2 cups all-purpose flour
3 tsp. baking powder
½ cup Dutch-process cocoa powder
¾ cups milk
1 tsp. vanilla extract

For the frosting
2 large-egg whites
1½ cup superfine sugar
pinch cream of tartar
pinch of salt
4 tbsp. water
a few drops pink food coloring
colored sugar, for sprinkling

TIP

To add to the decadence of these cupcakes, sprinkles should be added in a random fashion.

Preheat the oven to 350°F (175°C). Place 18 paper baking cups in muffin pans.

Beat the margarine and brown sugar in a medium bowl until pale and creamy. In a separate bowl beat the eggs. Gradually add the eggs to the creamed mixture a little at a time, beating well between each addition. Sift in the flour and cocoa, and fold the mixture until smooth. Slowly stir in the milk and vanilla.

Divide the mixture between the cups. Bake for 15–20 minutes until well risen and golden brown. Remove from the oven and cool for 5 minutes. Transfer to a wire rack to cool completely.

For the frosting, combine all the ingredients except the colored sugar in a bowl and beat using an electric mixer for 7–8 minutes, or until the mixture forms smooth peaks. Smooth frosting over the top of the cupcakes with the back of a teaspoon, then sprinkle over the colored sugar.

Store unfrosted in an airtight container for up to 3 days, or freeze for up to 3 months.

Makes 1¾ dozen

Marble Cupcakes

This simple two-tone cake is always a favorite with children who love the marbled effect when the cake is sliced. This version, topped with creamy frosting and chocolate chips, makes it even more appealing.

TIP

Omit the cocoa powder from half of the batter and instead tint it with pink food coloring for another kid-friendly recipe.

For the cupcakes
¾ cup (1½ sticks) sweet butter, at room temperature
¾ cup superfine sugar
3 extra-large eggs
scant 1¼ cups all-purpose flour
1 tsp. baking powder
1 tsp. vanilla extract
2 tbsp. unsweetened cocoa powder

For the frosting
⅓ cup (¾ stick) sweet butter, at room temperature
1¼ cups confectioners' sugar, sifted
1 tbsp. unsweetened cocoa powder, sifted
1–2 tbsp. milk
2 tbsp. semisweet chocolate chips, to decorate
2 tbsp. white chocolate chips, to decorate

Preheat the oven to 350°F (175°C). Line two 12-cup muffin pans with paper baking cups.

Beat together the butter and sugar until pale and creamy, then beat in the eggs one at a time. Sift the flour and the baking powder over the top, then fold in. Divide the mixture between two bowls. Stir the vanilla extract into one; sift the cocoa over the other bowl and fold in. Place alternating spoonfuls of the two batters in the paper cups so you finish with distinctive dollops of brown and white batter. Bake for 20–25 minutes until well risen and golden brown. Remove from the oven and cool for 5 minutes. Transfer to a wire rack to cool completely.

For the frosting, beat together the butter, sugar, cocoa, and 1 tablespoon milk until smooth. If necessary, add a little more milk, then spread over the cupcakes. Sprinkle with chocolate chips.

Makes 2 dozen

Magic Cupcakes

These funky magical cupcakes will brighten up any children's party.

For the cupcakes
1 cup (2 sticks) sweet butter, softened
1 cup superfine sugar
2 cups all-purpose flour
3 tsp. baking powder
4 large eggs
1 tsp. vanilla extract

For the frosting
3 cups confectioners' sugar, sifted
1 cup (2 sticks) sweet butter, softened
pinch of salt
pink food coloring
2 oz ready-to-roll white fondant sheet

TIP
You could try using red instead of pink food coloring and cutting out white fondant circles instead of stars—for a fun toadstool design.

Preheat the oven to 350°F (175°C). Place 18 paper baking cups in muffin pans. Combine all the cupcake ingredients in a large bowl and beat with an electric mixer until smooth and pale, about 2–3 minutes. Spoon the batter into the cups. Bake for 20 minutes. Remove pans from the oven and cool for 5 minutes. Then remove the cupcakes and cool on a rack.

To make the frosting, cream the confectioners' sugar, butter, and salt in a medium bowl with an electric mixer until smooth. Add a few drops of the food coloring, and mix until the frosting is a uniform bright pink. Cut small stars out of the fondant sheet. Pipe the pink frosting onto the cupcakes and place the white fondant stars on top.

Store unfrosted in an airtight container for up to 3 days, or freeze for up to 3 months.

Makes 1½ dozen

Chocolate Alphabet Cupcakes

Line these up to spell somebody's name at a birthday party!

For the cupcakes
1 cup (2 sticks) sweet butter, softened
1 cup superfine sugar
2 cups all-purpose flour
3 tsp. baking powder
4 large eggs
1 tsp. vanilla extract
½ cup (3½ oz) white chocolate chips

For the frosting
2 oz ready-to-roll white fondant sheet
3 tbsp. raspberry jelly
2 oz ready-to-roll red, green, and black fondant sheet
colored sprinkles

TIP

Why not try cutting out numbers rather than letters for a fun math experiment.

Preheat the oven to 350°F (175°C). Place 18 paper baking cups in muffin pans.

Combine all the cupcake ingredients, except the white chocolate chips, in a large bowl and beat with an electric mixer until smooth and pale, about 2–3 minutes. Stir in the white chocolate chips, then spoon the batter into the cups. Bake for 20 minutes. Remove pans from the oven and cool for 5 minutes. Then remove the cupcakes and cool on a rack.

For the frosting, roll out the white fondant and cut 18 circles using a 2-in. (5-cm) cookie cutter. Brush the cupcakes with a little of the jam. Press the circles onto the cupcakes. Using mini alphabet cutters, cut letter shapes from the colored fondant sheet and place them on top of the white circles. Sprinkle the edges with colored sprinkles.

Store unfrosted in an airtight container for up to 3 days, or freeze for up to 3 months.

Makes 1½ **dozen**

Sunny-side Up Cupcakes

Don't worry—you won't have to crack whole eggs to get this lovely sunny-side-up look. Serve these cupcakes for breakfast with a glass of freshly squeezed juice.

For the cupcakes
1 cup (2 sticks) sweet butter, softened
1 cup superfine sugar
2 cups all-purpose flour
3 tsp. baking powder
4 large eggs
1 tsp. vanilla extract

For the frosting
3 cups confectioners' sugar, sifted
1 cup (2 sticks) sweet butter, softened
pinch of salt
18 drained canned peach halves

TIP

For another fun look, replace the peach halves with gooseberries—for eyeball-style treats.

Preheat the oven to 350°F (175°C). Place 18 paper baking cups in muffin pans. Combine all the cupcake ingredients in a large bowl and beat with an electric mixer until smooth and pale, about 2–3 minutes. Spoon the batter into the cups. Bake for 20 minutes. Remove pans from the oven and cool for 5 minutes. Then remove the cupcakes and cool on a rack.

To make the frosting, put the confectioners' sugar, butter, and salt in a large bowl and beat with an electric mixer until smooth. Liberally spread the frosting onto the cooled cupcakes and garnish each cupcake with a peach half.

Store unfrosted in an airtight container for up to 3 days, or freeze for up to 3 months.

Makes 1½ dozen

Love-heart Cupcakes

These bright, loveable cupcakes will get the giggles started at any party.

For the cupcakes
1 cup (2 sticks) sweet butter, softened
1 cup superfine sugar
2 cups all-purpose flour
1½ tsp. baking powder
4 large eggs
1 tsp. vanilla extract

For the frosting
2 oz ready-to-roll light pink fondant sheet
2 oz ready-to-roll dark pink fondant sheet
3 tbsp. raspberry jelly

TIP

For a lovely effect, swap the colors over for each layer of fondant.

Preheat the oven to 350˚F (175˚C). Dust two cookie sheets with confectioners' sugar and put aside. Place 18 paper baking cups in muffin pans.

Combine all the cupcake ingredients in a large bowl and beat with an electric mixer until smooth and pale, about 2–3 minutes. Spoon the batter into the cups. Bake for 20 minutes. Remove pans from the oven and cool for 5 minutes. Then remove cupcakes and cool on a rack.

To make the frosting, roll the light pink fondant sheet to ⅛ in. (3 mm) thick. Cut 18 circles using a 2½-in. (6-cm) cookie cutter, and set them on one of the cookie sheets. Using a small heart-shaped cutter, cut out 18 mini hearts from the same fondant sheet. Roll the dark pink fondant sheet to ⅛ in. (3 mm) thick. Using a larger heart-shaped cutter, cut out 18 hearts and set them on the other cookie sheet. Brush each cupcake with a little jelly and lay a light pink circle on top. Place a large heart on top of the circle, and a small heart on top of that.

Store unfrosted in an airtight container for up to 3 days, or freeze for up to 3 months.

Makes 1½ **dozen**

Choc Candy-frosted Cupcakes

Candies are a kid's best friend. These little party cakes combine with a chocolate frosting for a real birthday treat which are fun to make and eat with the kids!

For the cupcakes
1 cup (2 sticks) sweet butter, softened
1 cup superfine sugar
2 cups all-purpose flour
3 tsp. baking powder
4 large eggs
1 tsp. vanilla extract

For the frosting
3½ oz semisweet chocolate, roughly chopped
2 tbsp. milk
¼ cup (½ stick) sweet butter
¾ cup confectioners' sugar, sifted
½ cup (3½ oz) lightly crushed chocolate candies

TIP
Make half using white chocolate instead of semisweet for an alternative taste.

Preheat the oven to 350°F (175°C). Place 18 paper baking cups in muffin pans.

Combine all the cupcake ingredients in a medium bowl and beat with an electric mixer until smooth and pale, about 2–3 minutes. Spoon the batter into the cups. Bake for 20 minutes. Remove the pans from the oven and cool for 5 minutes. Remove the cupcakes and cool on the rack.

To make the frosting, gently heat the chocolate, milk, and butter in a small, heavy saucepan, stirring until melted. Remove from the heat and beat in the confectioners' sugar. Stir in the chocolate candies, then swirl the frosting onto the cooled cupcakes.

Store unfrosted in an airtight container for up to 3 days, or freeze for up to 3 months.

Makes 1½ **dozen**

Choc Chip Florentine Cupcakes

Savor *la dolce vita* and get your kids to learn their Italian alphabet with these Italian-inspired cupcakes.

For the cupcakes
1 cup (2 sticks) sweet butter, softened
1 cup superfine sugar
2 cups all-purpose flour
3 tsp. baking powder
4 large eggs
1 tsp. vanilla extract
½ cup (3½ oz) semisweet chocolate chips

For the topping
3 tbsp. slivered almonds
3 tbsp. cornflakes
½ cup (3½ oz) roughly chopped candied cherries
3 tbsp. golden raisins
5 tbsp. condensed milk
2 oz semisweet chocolate, melted
2 oz white chocolate, melted

TIP

Add 3 tablespoons chopped candied cherries after creaming the batter for a fruitier flavor.

Preheat the oven to 350°F (175°C). Place 18 paper baking cups in muffin pans.

Combine all the cupcake ingredients except the chocolate chips in a large bowl and beat with an electric mixer until smooth and pale, about 2–3 minutes. Spoon the batter into the cups, then add the chocolate chips. Bake for 20 minutes. Remove pans from the oven and cool for 5 minutes. Then remove the cupcakes and cool on a rack.

For the florentine topping, combine all the ingredients except the chocolate in a small bowl. Spoon small teaspoons of the mixture onto silicone-lined cookie sheets. Bake for 5 minutes, until golden. Remove from the oven and cool for 1 minute. Remove the florentines from the sheet and crumble. Scatter over the cooled cupcakes and drizzle with the chocolate. Store in an airtight container for up to 2 days, or freeze for up to 3 months.

Makes 1½ **dozen**

Sparkling Fireworks Cupcakes

These cupcakes make a great dessert or centerpiece for any celebration. Serve them as they are or with whipped cream spooned over the top.

TIP

Silver dragées are illegal in some states, so only purchase them from reputable stores.

For the cupcakes
½ cup (1 stick) sweet butter
4½ oz bittersweet chocolate
6 large eggs, separated
1 tsp. vanilla extract
⅓ cup superfine sugar
1½ cups ground almonds

For the frosting
½ cup (3½ oz) bittersweet
    chocolate, chopped
generous ⅓ cup whipping cream
tiny multi-colored dragées and
    sparklers, to decorate

Preheat the oven to 325°F (160°C). Line two 12-cup muffin pans with paper baking cups.

Put butter and chocolate in a heatproof bowl over a pan of barely simmering water. Let it melt, stir until smooth, and set aside to cool for about 10 minutes.

Stir in egg yolks, vanilla, one-third of the sugar, and ground almonds. In a separate bowl, whisk the egg whites until they form soft peaks, then continue whisking, sprinkling the remaining sugar a tablespoon at a time over the whites, until stiff peaks form. Fold 2 tablespoons egg whites into the chocolate-almond mixture, then fold in the rest, one-third at a time.

Divide the mixture between the cups. Bake for 15–20 minutes until well risen and firm. Remove from the oven and cool for 5 minutes. Transfer to a wire rack to cool completely.

To make the frosting, put chocolate in a heatproof bowl. Heat cream until almost boiling, then pour it over the chocolate and let stand for about 5 minutes. Stir until smooth, then let cool until thick. Spread frosting over the cupcakes. To serve, sprinkle with silver dragées, stud each cake with mini indoor sparklers, and light. Store unfrosted in an airtight container for up to 2 days, or freeze for up to 3 months.

Makes 1½ dozen

Rocky Road Cupcakes

I'm not too sure how many will reach the table, but these simple no-bake cupcakes are great fun for the budding young chef to try.

1 cup (7 oz) bittersweet chocolate
¼ cup (½ stick) sweet butter, softened
5 tbsp. corn syrup
3 cups (3½ oz) crisp rice cereal
3 tbsp. chopped marshmallows

TIP

Stir in ½ cup raisins along with the cereal for a stickier, denser texture.

Line a 12-cup muffin pan with paper or foil baking cups.

Place the chocolate and butter in a double boiler or in a medium bowl over a pan of simmering water, and stir until melted. Remove pan from the heat and stir in the corn syrup, cereal, and marshmallows. Drop spoonfuls of the mixture into the cups and press down with the back of a spoon. Refrigerate for 1 hour.

Store in an airtight container for up to 5 days.

Makes 1 dozen

Peanut Butter & Jelly Cupcakes

Peanut butter and jelly are a classic combination—kids and grownups alike will find them hard to resist.

For the cupcakes
1 cup (2 sticks) sweet butter, softened
1 cup superfine sugar
2 tbsp. peanut butter
2 cups all-purpose flour
3 tsp. baking powder
4 large eggs, beaten

For the frosting
2 cups confectioners' sugar, sifted
¼ cup (½ stick) sweet butter
¼ cup peanut butter
½ cup strawberry jelly, to decorate

TIP

For a really nutty flavor, use thick, crunchy peanut butter. The frosting will not blend as smooth.

Preheat the oven to 350˚F (175˚C). Line a 24-cup mini muffin pan with paper baking cups.

Combine the butter, sugar, and peanut butter in a large bowl and beat with an electric mixer until smooth and pale, about 2–3 minutes. Fold in the sifted flour and baking powder and stir in the beaten eggs one at a time. Spoon the batter into the cups. Bake for 20 minutes. Remove pan from the oven and cool for 5 minutes. Then remove the cupcakes and cool on a rack.

To make the frosting, beat the confectioners' sugar, butter, and peanut butter using an electric mixer until smooth. Pipe the mixture in a swirl on top of each cupcake. Decorate with a dollop of strawberry jelly.

Store unfrosted in an airtight container for up to 2 days, or freeze for up to 3 months.

Makes 2 dozen

Chocolate Cupcakes

This is the ultimate collection of chocolate cupcakes. There is plenty here to tempt the most restrained of chocoholics.

Chocolate Cupcakes

Cupcake heaven would be incomplete without sumptuous chocolate cupcakes. Whether your chocoholic tendencies favor semisweet, milk, or white chocolate, you can make a wide array of creations guaranteed to satiate any cocoa craving. Choose from soft centers, rich frostings, chocolate and fruit combinations, or subtle bittersweet flavors.

The recipes in this chapter make perfect stand-alone snacks, but a range of serving suggestions prolong their shelf life and turn them into sensational desserts.

Chocolate Mud Cupcakes are soft and delicious the day you bake them, but storing in the refrigerator can turn the cake a little hard. Solve this problem easily by popping them in the microwave at full power for 30 seconds. Serve in a bowl with whipped cream or ice cream and sprinkle a little cocoa over the top. The same applies to the Chocolate Nougat Cupcakes. Warmed for a short amount of time and served sprinkled with cinnamon, these cupcakes stay mouthwatering even after days in the refrigerator. If you've decorated any cupcake with fresh fruit, avoid warming in the microwave. The chocolate creations are best eaten as soon as possible, but with these recipes, that's never a problem!

Chocolate Mud Cupcakes

These cupcakes are so simple to make you won't hesitate to make another batch.

1 cup (7 oz) semisweet
   chocolate chips
1⅓ cups (2¾ sticks) sweet butter
5 large eggs
⅔ cup superfine sugar
¾ cup all-purpose flour
1 tsp. baking powder
2 tbsp. Dutch-process cocoa
   powder, to decorate

TIP

Serve warm with chocolate fudge ice cream.

Preheat the oven to 325˚F (160˚C). Place 12 paper baking cups in a muffin pan.

In a double boiler, or a medium bowl set over a pan of gently simmering water, melt the chocolate and butter together, stirring well. Leave to cool a little.

Beat the eggs and sugar in a large bowl until pale and thick. Fold the flour and baking powder into the egg mixture and then stir in the melted chocolate and butter until well blended.

Spoon the mixture into the cups and bake for 20 minutes. The cupcakes will be soft and gooey in texture and appearance. Remove pan from the oven and cool for 5 minutes. Then remove the cupcakes from the pan. Serve swiftly, dusted with cocoa powder.

Store in the refrigerator in an airtight container for up to 3 days. Suitable for freezing.

Makes 1 dozen

Triple Chocolate Cupcakes

For the best texture, take care not to overmix the batter—just stir until the mixture comes together. A few lumps are fine!

5 oz semisweet chocolate
3¼ cups all-purpose flour
1 tbsp. baking powder
½ cup Dutch-process cocoa powder
⅓ cup superfine sugar
2 extra-large eggs
2 tsp. vanilla extract
6 tbsp. sunflower oil

1½ cups milk
5 oz milk chocolate, roughly chopped
5 oz white chocolate, roughly chopped

TIP

Why not add a chocolate glaze for a quadruple chocolate cupcake?

Preheat the oven to 400°F (200°C). Line two 12-muffin pans with 24 paper baking cups.

Melt the semisweet chocolate in a double boiler. Sift together the flour, baking powder, and cocoa into a medium bowl and stir in the sugar. In a separate bowl beat the eggs, vanilla, oil, and milk. Stir in the melted chocolate. Stir the chocolate mixture into the flour and add the chopped chocolate.

Divide the mixture between the muffin cups and bake for 20–25 minutes until well risen. Remove from the oven and transfer to a wire rack. Dust with confectioners' sugar before serving. Serve warm or cold.

Store in an airtight container for up to 4 days. Suitable for freezing.

Makes 2 dozen

Oreo-filled Chocolate Cupcakes

Oreos are everyone's favorite cookies—why not make a batch of these for a particularly hardcore fan?

For the cupcakes
2 cups (4 sticks) sweet butter, softened
8 oz caster sugar
2 cups all-purpose flour
3 tsp. baking powder
4 tbsp. Dutch-processed cocoa powder
4 large eggs
1 tsp. vanilla extract

For the frosting
1 envelope unflavored gelatin
½ cup cold water
1 cup Crisco
1 tsp. vanilla
4 cups confectioners' sugar

TIP

The gelatin is used to give the filling stability.

Preheat the oven to 350°F (175°C). Line muffin pans with 18 paper baking cups.

Combine the cupcake ingredients in a large bowl and beat with an electric whisk until smooth, about 2–3 minutes. Spoon the batter into the cases. Bake for 20 minutes. Remove pans from the oven and cool for 5 minutes. Then remove the cupcakes and cool on a rack.

To make the frosting, soften the gelatin in the cold water. Place in a heatproof cup in a pan of hot water until gelatin is transparent. Meanwhile beat Crisco until fluffy, adding vanilla and sugar a little at a time. Cool the gelatin mixture, then beat into the Crisco mixture straightaway. Shape into 18 1-in. balls. Cut out a small disk from the top of each cupcake. Spoon in a teaspoon of the oreo-flavored icing, and add the removed disk of cupcake on the top.

Store in the refrigerator in an airtight container for up to 3 days. Suitable for freezing.

Makes 1½ dozen

Chocolate–mint Cupcakes

This glaze will work wonderfully on a number of the other cakes in this book—sticky, minty, and delicious.

For the cupcakes
2 cups all-purpose flour
3 tsp. baking powder
¼ tsp. salt
3 tbsp. Dutch-process cocoa powder
¾ cup (1½ sticks) sweet butter, softened
1½ cups superfine sugar
3 extra-large eggs

2 tsp peppermint essence
1 cup milk

For the glaze
3 oz plain chocolate
2 oz butter
1 tsp. peppermint essence

TIP
Try spearmint for an ultra-refreshing take on the recipe.

Preheat the oven to 350°F (175°C). Line 20 deep muffin or bun pans with paper cups.

Sift together the flour, baking soda, salt and cocoa powder. In a second large bowl, using an electric mixer, beat the butter and sugar until light and creamy, about 5 minutes. Add the eggs, one at a time, beating well after each addition, then beat in the peppermint essence. On low speed, beat in the flour mixture alternately with the milk just until blended. Stir the flour mixture into the butter mixture. Spoon into paper cups, filling each about three-quarters full.

Bake for 12–15 minutes, until a fine skewer inserted in the center come out clean; do not over bake. Cool in the tins on a wire rack to cool completely. Meanwhile, prepare the glaze. In a saucepan over low heat, melt the chocolate and butter, stirring until smooth. Remove from the heat and stir in the essence. Cool until spreadable, then spread on top of each cake.

Store unfrosted in the refrigerator in an airtight container for up to 3 days. Suitable for freezing.

Makes 18–20

Chocolate Butterfly Cupcakes

These utterly fluttery cakes feel light as a feather—but don't be fooled as they are seriously luxurious.

For the cupcakes
½ cup (1 stick) butter or
   margarine
1 cup granulated sugar
2 extra-large eggs
1 tsp. grated orange rind
4 oz semisweet chocolate,
   finely grated
1¼ cups all-purpose flour
1¼ tsp. baking powder

For the frosting
½ cup (1 stick) sweet butter
   (or margarine)
1⅔ cups confectioners' sugar,
   sifted
3 oz semisweet chocolate, melted
confectioners' sugar and seedless
   candied cherries, to decorate

TIP

You could top with raspberry jelly instead of the candied cherries.

Preheat the oven to 350˚F (175˚C). Line 18 deep muffin or bun pans with paper cases.

Put the butter and sugar in a bowl and cream until light and puffy. Beat the eggs a little at a time. Stir in the orange rind and chocolate. Then fold in the flour and baking powder. Divide the mixture between the cases. Bake for about 15–20 minutes. Let cool.

To make the frosting, beat together the butter and confectioners' sugar. Then gradually beat in the cooled, melted chocolate. Starting ¼-in. from the edge, remove the top of each cake by cutting in and slightly down to form a cavity. Pipe a little frosting in the cavity of each cake. Sprinkle the reserved cake tops with confectioners' sugar and cut each one in half.

Place each half, cut outward, on to the frosting to form wings. Pipe small rosettes of frosting in the center of each cake. Top with a candied cherry.

Store unfrosted in the refrigerator in an airtight container for up to 3 days. Suitable for freezing.

Makes 1½ dozen

Chocolate Maltie Cupcakes

A classic recipe for a classic cupcake craving…

3 oz semisweet chocolate
3 oz cream cheese
¼ cup (½ stick) butter
   (or margarine)
1 tbsp. instant malt milk powder
½ tsp. vanilla extract
3 cups confectioners' sugar, sieved

½ cup milk
1⅓ cups all-purpose flour
1½ tsp. baking powder
2 extra-large eggs
chocolate buttons, to decorate

TIP

Serve with a malted vanilla shake for a real nostalgic snack.

Preheat the oven to 350°F (175°C). Line 24 deep muffin or bun pans with paper cups.

Melt the chocolate and allow to cool slightly. Beat together the cream cheese, butter, malted milk powder, and vanilla. Beat in the confectioners' sugar and half the milk alternately. Beat in the melted chocolate. Remove 8 oz of the chocolate mixture. Cover and reserve for the frosting.

Sift together the flour and the baking powder. Beat in the eggs. Stir in the flour alternately with the remaining milk. Fill the cups two-thirds full with the mixture. Bake in the oven for about 20 minutes. Cool.

To serve, ice the cakes with the reserved chocolate frosting. Decorate with chocolate buttons if you wish.

Store unfrosted in the refrigerator in an airtight container for up to 3 days. Suitable for freezing.

Makes 2 dozen

Chocolate & Cinnamon Brioches

You'll find yourself drawn to the breakfast table by the aroma of these sweet breads, a perfect accompaniment to steaming hot coffee.

½ tbsp. active dry yeast
½ cup warm water
1 tsp. granulated sugar
2½ cups all-purpose flour
3 tsp. baking powder
2 tsp. cinnamon
4 large eggs
¼ cup superfine sugar

pinch of salt
½ cup (1 stick) sweet butter, softened
½ cup (3½ oz) raisins
½ cup (3½ oz) semisweet chocolate chips
1 large beaten egg

TIP

If you add a pinch of saffron to the dry ingredients you can get a lovely fragrant flavor.

Combine the yeast, water, and the teaspoon of sugar in a large bowl. Stir well and leave in a warm place for 10 minutes. Stir in ½ cup of the flour and the cinnamon until the mixture becomes a smooth paste. Beat the eggs and add them to the yeast mixture. Add the sugar and salt. Stir in the remaining flour and the baking powder, and mix until the dough is soft and slightly sticky. Leave in a warm place, covered with plastic wrap, for 45 minutes or until doubled in bulk.

Preheat the oven to 400°F (200°C). Grease 12 mini brioche or muffin molds. Beat in the butter, raisins, and chocolate chips. Fill the molds halfway. Leave in a warm place for about 20 minutes, until the dough has risen to fill about two-thirds of each mold.

Brush each brioche with a little of the beaten egg and bake for 20 minutes. Cool in the molds for 5 minutes, remove, and cool on a rack. Store in an airtight container for up to 2 days.

Makes 1 dozen

White Choc Chip & Orange Cupcakes

Orange extract helps sweeten the bitterness of the chocolate.

For the cupcakes
1 cup (2 sticks) sweet butter, softened
1 cup superfine sugar
2 cups all-purpose flour
3 tsp. baking powder
4 large eggs
1 tsp. orange extract
½ cup (3½ oz) white chocolate chips

For the glaze
½ cup (3½ oz) semisweet chocolate chips
⅓ cup heavy cream
1 tsp. orange extract

TIP

Replace all the semisweet chocolate chips in the recipe for white ones for a milkier chocolate delight.

Preheat the oven to 350°F (175°C). Place 18 paper baking cups in muffin pans.

Combine all the cupcake ingredients, except the chocolate chips, in a large bowl and beat with an electric mixer until smooth and pale, about 2–3 minutes. Stir in the chocolate chips. Spoon the batter into the cups. Bake for 20 minutes. Remove pans from the oven and cool for 5 minutes. Then remove the cupcakes and cool on a rack.

For the chocolate glaze, melt the chocolate in a double boiler or medium bowl over a pan of simmering water, stirring until completely melted. Add the cream and orange extract, and stir until well combined. Cool slightly and pour over the cupcakes. Refrigerate until set.

Store unfrosted in an airtight container for up to 2 days, or freeze for up to 3 months.

Makes 1½ dozen

Chocolate & Black Pepper Cupcakes

Black pepper, chocolate, and strawberries are a very sophisticated flavor trio. Try a dusting of freshly grounded pepper on top for an extra spicy taste.

TIP

Replace the black pepper with chili pepper flakes for a spicy alternative.

For the cupcakes
1 cup (2 sticks) sweet butter, softened
1 cup superfine sugar
2 cups all-purpose flour
3 tsp. baking powder
4 large eggs
1 tsp. strawberry extract
½ cup (3½ oz) semisweet chocolate chips
1 tsp. freshly ground black pepper

For the frosting
1 cup cream cheese, softened
1½ cups confectioners' sugar, sifted
1 tsp. vanilla extract
3 tbsp. sweet butter, softened
3 tbsp. chopped fresh strawberries

Preheat the oven to 350°F (175°C). Place 18 paper baking cups in muffin pans.

Combine the butter, sugar, flour, baking powder, eggs, and strawberry extract in a medium bowl. Beat with an electric mixer until light and creamy, about 2–3 minutes. Stir in the chocolate chips and black pepper. Spoon the batter into the cups. Bake for 20 minutes. Remove pans from the oven and cool for 5 minutes. Then remove the cupcakes and cool on a rack.

To make the frosting, beat the cream cheese, confectioners' sugar, vanilla, and butter until smooth and creamy. Stir in the chopped strawberries. Spread frosting on top of the cupcakes.

Store unfrosted in an airtight container for up to 2 days, or freeze for up to 3 months.

Makes 1½ dozen

White Choc & Vanilla Cupcakes

These vanilla cupcakes are giving a slightly different texture with the crunchy addition of white chocolate chips.

For the cupcakes
1 cup (2 sticks) sweet butter, softened
1 cup superfine sugar
2 cups all-purpose flour
3 tsp. baking powder
4 large eggs
1 tsp. vanilla extract
½ cup (3½ oz) white choc chips

Preheat the oven to 350°F (175°C). Place 18 paper baking cups into muffin pans.

Combine all the cupcake ingredients except the choc chips in a medium bowl and beat with an electric mixer until smooth and pale, about 2–3 minutes. Stir in the choc chips, then spoon the batter into the cups. Bake for 20 minutes. Remove the pans from the oven and cool for 5 minutes. Remove the cupcakes and cool on the rack.

Makes 1½ **dozen**

TIP

Raisins or chopped prunes work well in these cupcakes too, just replace the chocolate chips.

Mocha Chocolate Cupcakes

These melt-in-the-mouth cupcakes with their soft, mousse-like center are a truly decadent treat. Serve them with a cup of coffee when you need a pick-me-up or savor them for dessert.

TIP

For an alcoholic kick, replace the coffee with 2 tablespoons Amaretto liqueur.

9 oz bittersweet chocolate
¾ cup (1½ sticks) butter, diced
1 cup superfine sugar
3 extra-large eggs
generous ⅔ cup all-purpose flour
1 tsp. baking powder
2 tbsp. instant coffee dissolved in
   2 tbsp. boiling water
heavy cream, to serve
12 strawberries, halved

Preheat the oven to 325°F (160°C). Line two 12-cup muffin pans with paper baking cups.

Break the chocolate into pieces and put them in a heatproof bowl with the butter. Place the bowl over a pan of gently simmering water and heat gently until the chocolate and butter have melted. Remove from the heat and let cool for 5 minutes.

Stir in the sugar, then beat in the eggs, one at a time. Sift the flour over the mixture, then fold in. Stir in the coffee. Divide the mixture between the cups. Bake for 15–20 minutes until risen and just set. Remove from the oven and cool completely. Transfer to a wire rack to cool completely.

Serve dotted with spoonfuls of heavy cream and a piece of strawberry. Store unfrosted in an airtight container for up to 2 days, or freeze for up to 3 months.

Makes 2 dozen

Chocolate Pound Cupcakes

This is one of the all-time classic simple cakes that has been enjoyed for generations. Originally the cake was made with a pound each of butter, sugar, eggs, and flour—hence its name.

⅔ cup (1⅔ sticks) sweet butter, at
    room temperature
1⅔ cups superfine sugar
6 large eggs
2½ cups all-purpose flour
1½ tsp. baking powder
4 tbsp. unsweetened cocoa powder,
    plus extra to dust
4 tbsp. milk
1 tsp. vanilla extract

TIP

Add ½ cup roughly chopped walnuts to the cake mixture for added sustenance.

Preheat the oven to 325°F (160°C). Line two 12-cup muffin pans with paper baking cups.

Beat together the butter and sugar until pale and creamy, then beat in the eggs one at a time. Sift the flour baking powder, and cocoa powder over the mixture, then fold in. Stir in the milk and vanilla.

Divide the mixture between the cups. Bake for 15–20 minutes until well risen and golden brown. Remove from the oven and cool for 5 minutes. Transfer to a wire rack to cool completely.

Cool in the pan for 5 minutes, then transfer to a wire rack to cool completely. Before serving, dust lightly with cocoa powder. Store unfrosted in an airtight container for up to 2 days, or freeze for up to 3 months.

Makes 2 dozen

Chocolate Ginger Cupcakes

Nothing quite beats a rich, dark ginger cake and these cupcakes are sure to satisfy a craving—delicious with mug of hot tea.

For the cupcakes
3⅓ cups all-purpose flour
½ tsp. salt
1 tbsp. baking powder
1 tsp. baking soda
2 tsp. ground ginger
¾ cup dark molasses
¾ cup light corn syrup
¾ cup (1½ sticks) butter, diced
generous ¾ cup milk

3 pieces of stem ginger in syrup,
  roughly chopped

For the frosting
1 cup cream cheese, softened
1½ cups confectioners' sugar, sifted
3 tbsp. sweet butter, softened
2 tsp. finely chopped stem ginger

TIP

These cakes will be even better a few days after baking; so if you can, make them a few days in advance, wrap tightly, and store in an airtight container until ready to frost and serve.

Preheat the oven to 350°F (175°C). Line two 12-cup muffin pans with paper baking cups.

Combine the flour, salt, baking powder, baking soda, and ginger. Sift into a large bowl. Make a well in the middle.

Put the molasses, corn syrup, and butter in a pan and warm gently until the butter has melted and the mixture is smooth and combined. Stir in the milk and stem ginger. Pour the mixture into the well in the middle of the dry ingredients. Mix well to make a smooth batter.

Divide the mixture between the cups. Bake for 20 minutes until well risen and golden brown. Remove from the oven and cool for 5 minutes. Transfer to a wire rack to cool completely. Let cakes cool in the pan for about 10 minutes, then transfer to a wire rack to cool completely.

To make the frosting, beat the cream cheese, confectioners' sugar, butter, and chopped ginger until smooth and creamy. Spread over the top of the cupcakes.

Makes 2 dozen

Chocolate Cherry Marzipan Cupcakes

Layering the cupcakes with marzipan gives them a lusciously sticky and indulgent center.

¾ cup (1½ sticks) butter, at
    room temperature
¾ cup superfine sugar
3 extra-large eggs
scant 1¼ cups all-purpose flour
1½ tsp. baking powder

scant 1 cup ground almond
½ cup candied cherries, chopped
½ cup chopped bittersweet
    chocolate
4 oz marzipan, finely grated
confectioners' sugar, to decorate

TIP

These cupcakes are particularly good served warm for afternoon tea or morning coffee.

Preheat the oven to 350°F (175°C). Line two 12-cup muffin pans with paper baking cups.

Beat together the butter and sugar until pale and creamy, then beat in the eggs one at a time. Sift the flour, baking powder, and ground almonds over the mixture, then fold in. Scatter the cherries and chocolate over the mixture, then fold in until evenly distributed.

Divide half the mixture between the cups to come halfway up the sides. Sprinkle the marzipan on top. Spoon over the remaining batter and smooth out evenly. Bake for 20–25 minutes until golden.

Let the cupcakes cool in the pans for about 10 minutes, then lift out onto a wire rack to cool. Serve slightly warm from the oven or at room temperature, dusted with confectioners' sugar.

Makes 2 dozen

Chocolate Meringue-topped Cupcakes

A chocolatey take on the classic key lime pie. These cupcakes look great and taste even better!

For the cupcakes
1 cup (2 sticks) sweet butter, softened
1 cup superfine sugar
2 cups all-purpose flour
3 tsp. baking powder
4 large eggs
1 tsp. vanilla extract

For the filling
½ cup (3½ oz) semisweet chocolate chips

For the meringue
3 large egg whites
¼ tsp. cream of tartar
⅓ cup granulated sugar

TIP
Dust with cinnamon for an added zing.

Preheat the oven to 350˚F (175˚C). Place 18 paper baking cups in muffin pans.

Place all the cupcake ingredients in a large bowl, and beat with an electric mixer until smooth and pale, about 2–3 minutes. Spoon the batter into the cups. Bake for 20 minutes. Remove pans from the oven and cool for 5 minutes. Then remove the cupcakes and cool on a rack.

For the filling, melt the chocolate chips in a double boiler and cool slightly. Remove the top from each cupcake and hollow out a small hole. Spoon the filling into the hole and replace the top. Refrigerate until set.

Preheat the oven to 450˚F (230˚C). For the meringue, beat the eggs and cream of tartar until soft peaks form. Add one-third of the sugar and beat for 1 minute. Repeat until all the sugar has been added. Spoon or pipe the meringue on top of the cupcakes. Bake for 5 minutes until golden.

Store for no more than 1 day in an airtight container.

Makes 1½ **dozen**

Chocolate Nougat Cupcakes

These delightful cupcakes contain a rich and gooey caramel surprise.

½ cup (1 stick) sweet butter, softened
¾ cup packed brown sugar
2 lightly beaten extra-large eggs
2 tbsp. instant coffee granules
1 tbsp. boiling water
2⅔ cups all-purpose flour
3¼ tsp. baking powder
½ cup milk
12 Hershey's Caramel Kisses

TIP

The Caramel Kisses could be replaced with other small caramel chocolates candies.

Preheat the oven to 350°F (175°C). Place 12 paper baking cups in a muffin pan.

In a medium bowl, beat the butter and sugar until pale and creamy. Add the eggs slowly. In a small bowl, dissolve the coffee in the water. Beat the coffee into the butter mixture. Add the flour, baking powder, and milk, and beat until well combined.

Spoon the mixture into the cups. Push the Caramel Kisses into the center of each cupcake, and place them in the oven. Bake for 20 minutes. Cool for 5 minutes in the pan. Turn onto a plate and serve while warm.

Store in an airtight container for up to 2 days.

Makes 1 dozen

Truffle-topped Chocolate Cupcakes

Like the traditional cherry, this truffle sits on top of the cupcake—a rich addition to a simple recipe. The question is, how do you eat yours?

For the cupcakes
⅔ cup butter
½ cup sugar
2 extra-large eggs
1 tsp. vanilla extract
1¾ cups all-purpose flour
2 tbsp. cocoa powder
2 tsp. baking powder
8 tbsp. milk

For the frosting
1 egg white
1½ cups confectioners' sugar
12 small chocolate truffles

TIP

You could try making your own truffles for a real treat.

Preheat the oven to 350°F (180°C) and line a muffin pan with 12 paper cups.

Cream the butter until light and fluffy, then one after the other beat in the sugar, eggs, and vanilla extract. Mix the flour, baking powder, and cocoa and add to the creamed mixture with the milk, alternating additions of dry ingredients and milk. Spoon into the prepared paper cases and bake for 25–30 minutes. Take out of the oven, let cool slightly in the pan, then take out and cool on a cake rack.

To make the frosting, beat the egg white until semi-stiff, then mix with the confectioners' sugar to make a smooth, thick frosting. Put a little of the frosting on each cupcake, decorate with a chocolate truffle, and let dry before serving.

Store in an airtight container for up to 2 days. Freeze for up to 3 months.

Makes 1 dozen

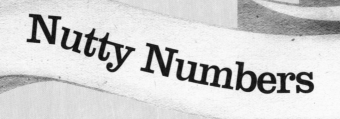

Nutty Numbers

Creamy, crunchy, and smooth are just some
of the ways you could describe these
nut-packed cupcakes. Choose from flavors
that include pecan and maple, peanut butter,
and caramel nut crunch.

Nutty Numbers

Nutty numbers strike a chord with cupcake lovers everywhere. The variety of flavors and textures will tantalize your tastebuds, and nutty cupcakes can make filling snacks as well as healthy additions to your diet, as hearty comfort cupcakes, or light and fluffy morsels. It may be tempting to substitute nuts in the recipe for your particular favorite, but try the original cupcake first; you may be surprised by the flavor combinations.

Pecans go well with sweet and sticky foods; that's why rich and heavy pecan pie is always so good. Almonds on the other hand are perfect on their own, with a vanilla cupcake batter, or with cherries for that traditional "bakewell tart" taste. Walnuts are an excellent source of omega 3, and they combine well with bittersweet flavors like dark chocolate and coffee. Pistachio nuts have a strong impact on cupcake recipes, so pairing them with mild flavors like vanilla or rosewater works best. Similarly, hazelnuts have a potent flavor that goes well with fruit in cupcakes. Enjoy the recipes in this chapter and then try your own nutty number creations.

Maple Syrup, Date & Pecan Cupcakes

With over 40 different named varieties, the date fruit of the palm tree comes in many different textures and flavors.

For the cupcakes
2½ cups all-purpose flour
¾ cup superfine sugar
1 tbsp. baking powder
2 extra-large eggs
4 tbsp. butter, melted
¼ cup soured cream
2 tbsp. milk
1 large mashed banana

1 cup (6 oz) chopped dates, plus
    extra to decorate
4 tbsp. chopped pecans

For the maple syrup butter
2 tbsp. maple syrup
½ cup (1 stick) sweet butter,
    softened

TIP
For these cupcakes try using Medjool dates, which have a thick flesh and a dark, rich flavor.

Preheat the oven to 350°F (175°C). Line a 12-cup muffin pan with paper baking cups.

In a medium bowl, combine the flour, sugar, and baking powder with a spoon. In a large bowl, beat the eggs, butter, sour cream, milk, and banana with an electric mixer until combined. Fold in the flour mixture until just combined. Stir in the dates and pecan nuts.

Spoon the mixture into the prepared pan. Bake for 20 minutes. Remove pan from the oven and cool for 5 minutes. Then remove the cakes and cool on a rack.

For the maple syrup butter, combine the maple syrup and butter in a bowl. Spread over the top of the cooled cupcakes. Decorate with chopped dates.

Store in an airtight container for up to 3 days, or freeze for up to 3 months without frosting.

Makes 1 dozen

Almond Cupcakes

Easy to make, these little cakes with their delicate almond flavor are a mouthwatering treat.

1 cup (2 sticks) sweet butter, softened
1 cup superfine sugar
2 cups all-purpose flour
3 tsp. baking powder

4 large eggs
2 drops vanilla extract
4 tbsp. almonds, grated
4 tbsp. flaked toasted almonds, to serve

TIP

For a special occasion, soak the cakes in sherry or freshly squeezed orange juice with a little rum added, then top with whipped cream.

Preheat the oven to 350°F (175°C). Place 18 paper baking cups in muffin pans.

Combine all the cupcake ingredients except the almonds in a medium bowl and beat with an electric mixer until smooth and pale, about 2–3 minutes. Stir in the almonds, then spoon the batter into the cups. Bake for 20 minutes. Remove pans from the oven and cool for 5 minutes. Then remove the cupcakes and cool on a rack.

Store unfrosted for up to 3 days in an airtight container, or freeze for 3 months.

Makes 1½ dozen

Walnut & Coffee-frosted Cupcakes

Carrot cake can be adapted easily to become a real treat instead of an everyday staple. Walnut and coffee varieties work wonderfully well and taste delicious with a cappuccino on a cold day.

For the cupcakes
1 cup (2 sticks) sweet butter, softened
1 cup superfine sugar
2 cups all-purpose flour
3 tsp. baking powder
4 large eggs
1 tsp. allspice
1 cup (3½ oz) chopped walnuts
1 cup freshly shredded carrot
2 tbsp. golden raisins

For the frosting
1 cup cream cheese, softened
1½ cups confectioners' sugar, sifted
1 tsp. hot coffee
1 tsp. instant coffee granules
1 tsp. coffee liqueur
3 tbsp. chopped walnuts

TIP

You could replace the cream cheese with mascarpone for a different take on the recipe.

Preheat the oven to 350°F (175°C). Place 18 baking cups in muffin pans.

Combine the butter, sugar, flour, and eggs in a large bowl and beat with an electric mixer until smooth, about 2–3 minutes. Stir in the rest of the ingredients. Spoon the batter into the cups. Bake for 20 minutes. Remove pans from the oven and cool for 5 minutes. Then remove the cupcakes and cool on a rack.

To make the frosting, slowly beat the cream cheese and confectioners' sugar in a large bowl with an electric mixer until creamy and soft. Mix in the hot coffee, granules, and liqueur. Spread the frosting liberally onto the cooled cupcakes and garnish with the chopped walnuts.

Store unfrosted for up to 3 days in an airtight container, or freeze for up to 3 months.

Makes 1½ dozen

Fudge-frosted Peanut Butter Cupcakes

The texture of crunchy peanut butter in this recipe is excellent, though creamier varieties also work.

For the cupcakes
1 cup (2 sticks) sweet butter, softened
1 cup superfine sugar
2 cups all-purpose flour
3 tsp. baking powder
4 large eggs
1 cup crunchy peanut butter

For the frosting
½ cup smooth peanut butter
½ cup (1 stick) sweet butter, softened
2 tsp. vanilla extract
2 cups confectioners' sugar, sifted
2 tbsp. milk
2 tbsp. Dutch-process cocoa powder

TIP
Try adding ½ cup semisweet chocolate chips to the batter.

Preheat the oven to 350°F (175°C). Place 18 paper baking cups in muffin pans.

Combine the butter, sugar, flour, baking powder, and eggs in a large bowl and beat with an electric mixer until smooth, about 2–3 minutes. Stir in the peanut butter until well combined. Spoon the batter into the cups. Bake for 20 minutes. Remove pans from the oven and cool for 5 minutes. Then remove the cupcakes and cool on a rack.

To make the frosting, combine the peanut butter, butter, and vanilla in a medium bowl. Using an electric mixer beat until light and fluffy, about 1–2 minutes. Add the confectioners' sugar along with the milk, and beat until well combined. Then beat in the the cocoa. Spread the frosting onto the cooled cupcakes.

Store unfrosted in an airtight container for up to 3 days, or freeze for up to 3 months.

Makes 1 ½ dozen

Hazelnut & Raisin Butterfly Cupcakes

A nutty take on a classic cupcake, which can be served with tea or as a dessert.

For the cupcakes
1 cup (2 sticks) sweet butter, softened
1 cup superfine sugar
2 cups all-purpose flour
3 tsp. baking powder
4 large eggs
1 tsp. vanilla extract

For the frosting
½ cup (1 stick) sweet butter
2 cups confectioners' sugar, sifted
1 tsp. vanilla extract
1 tbsp. lemon zest
3 tbsp. roughly chopped toasted hazelnuts
2 tbsp. golden raisins

TIP
Lime zest can also be substituted for a sharper flavor.

Preheat the oven to 350˚F (175˚C). Place 18 paper baking cups in muffin pans.

Combine all ingredients for the cupcakes in a large bowl and beat with an electric mixer until smooth and pale, about 2–3 minutes. Spoon the batter into the cups. Bake for 20 minutes. Remove pans from the oven and cool for 5 minutes. Then remove the cupcakes and cool on a rack.

Prepare the frosting by beating the butter, confectioners' sugar, vanilla, and lemon zest until smooth. Cut a slice from the top of each cake and cut it into two. Pipe or spoon the frosting onto the flattened top of each cupcake. Then place the half-circles of cake at an angle on each side of the frosting. Decorate with the hazelnuts and raisins.

Store unfrosted in an airtight container for up to 3 days, or freeze for up to 3 months.

Makes 1½ **dozen**

Cherry & Almond Cupcakes

This Bakewell-style cupcake with a kirsch kick is pure decadence.

TIP

You could also decorate with 2 tablespoons chopped toasted almonds.

For the cupcakes
1 cup (2 sticks) sweet butter, softened
1 cup superfine sugar
2 cups all-purpose flour
3 tbsp. ground almonds
3 tsp. baking powder
4 large eggs
2 tbsp. kirsch

For the frosting
3 cups confectioners' sugar, sifted
1 cup (2 sticks) sweet butter
pinch of salt
red food coloring
12 bottled morello or maraschino cherries with stems, to decorate

Preheat the oven to 350°F (175°C). Place 18 paper baking cups in muffin pans.

Combine all the cupcake ingredients in a large bowl and beat with an electric mixer until smooth, about 2–3 minutes. Spoon the batter into the cups.

Bake for 20 minutes. Remove pans from the oven and cool for 5 minutes. Then remove the cupcakes and cool on a rack.

To make the frosting, beat the confectioners' sugar, butter, and salt in a medium bowl with an electric mixer until smooth. Add a few drops of the food coloring and beat until well combined and pink. Spread the frosting onto the cooled cupcakes, and garnish each with a cherry.

Store in an airtight container for up to 3 days, or freeze unfrosted for up to 3 months.

Makes 1 ½ dozen

Pistachio & Rosewater Cupcakes

The delicate and sweet flavor of the rosewater works wonderfully with the salty contrast of the pistachio nuts.

For the cupcakes
1 cup (2 sticks) sweet butter, softened
1 cup superfine sugar
2 cups all-purpose flour
3 tsp. baking powder
4 large eggs
1 tsp. rosewater

For the frosting
1 cup cream cheese
1½ cups confectioners' sugar, sifted
2 tbsp. rosewater
3 tbsp. pistachios, roughly chopped

TIP

Add a pinch of saffron to the dry ingredients for a lovely fragrant flavor and a brilliant yellow color.

Preheat the oven to 350°F (175°C). Place 18 paper baking cups in muffin pans.

Combine all the cupcake ingredients in a medium bowl and beat with an electric mixer until smooth and pale, about 2–3 minutes.

Spoon the batter into the cups. Bake for 20 minutes. Remove pans from the oven and cool for 5 minutes. Then remove the cupcakes and cool on a rack.

For the frosting, combine the cream cheese and confectioners' sugar, and beat with an electric mixer until soft and creamy. Add the rosewater, and stir well. Swirl onto the top of the cupcakes. Add the pistachios on top.

Store unfrosted for up to 3 days in an airtight container, or freeze for up to 3 months.

Makes 1½ **dozen**

Maple, Pecan & Walnut-frosted Cupcakes

The hearty flavor of these cupcakes is perfect for tailgate and fall picnics.

For the cupcakes
¾ cup (1½ sticks) butter, at room
   temperature
¾ cup superfine sugar
3 extra-large eggs
scant 1¼ cups all-purpose flour
1½ tsp. baking powder
½ cup pecans, roughly chopped

For the frosting
1 cup cream cheese, softened
½ cup (1 stick) sweet butter,
   softened
1½ cups confectioners' sugar, sifted
½ tsp. maple-flavored extract
½ cup (3½ oz) chopped walnuts

TIP
You could replace the frosting with a coffee-flavored one (see page 108 for a recipe).

Preheat the oven to 350°F (175°C). Place 18 paper baking cups in muffin pans.

Beat the butter and sugar together until pale and creamy, then beat in the eggs one at a time. Sift the flour and baking powder over the egg mixture, then fold in. Add the pecans and fold in.

Tip the mixture into the prepared cups. Bake for 20–25 minutes until golden and well risen.

Let cool in the pan for about 20 minutes, then turn out onto a wire rack to cool completely.

To make the frosting, beat the cream cheese and butter together with an electric mixer, until light and fluffy. Add the confectioners' sugar and beat until creamy. Beat in the maple-flavored extract. Spread the frosting on the cupcakes and scatter over the walnuts.

Store unfrosted in an airtight container for up to 3 days, or freeze for up to 3 months.

Makes 1½ dozen

Peach & Almond Cupcakes

Slivered almonds add texture to this mouthwateringly peachy, delightful little cupcake.

1 cup (2 sticks) sweet butter, softened
1 cup superfine sugar
2 cups all purpose flour
3 tsp. baking powder

4 large eggs
drop vanilla extract
2 oz canned peaches
4 tbsp. slivered almonds

Preheat the oven to 350°F (175°C). Place 18 paper baking cups in muffin pans.

Combine all the cupcake ingredients except the peaches and slivered almonds in a medium bowl and beat with an electric mixer until smooth and pale, about 2–3 minutes.

Stir in the peaches and slivered almonds, then spoon the batter into the cups. Bake for 20 minutes. Remove pans from the oven and cool for 5 minutes. Then remove the cupcakes and cool on a rack.

Store unfrosted for up to 3 days in an airtight container, or freeze for 3 months.

Makes 1½ dozen

TIP

Use the syrup from the can to make frosting. Mix with confectioner's sugar for a wonderfully peachy glaze.

Nutty Hummingbird Cupcakes

You'll love this nutty variation of this classic cupcake from the American South.

For the cupcakes
1¼ cups all-purpose flour
1½ tsp. baking powder
½ tsp. cinnamon
¾ cup superfine sugar
½ cup safflower oil
2 extra-large eggs
½ cup chopped macadamia nuts,
    plus extra for decorating
½ cup (2 medium) mashed bananas
1½ tbsp. grated orange zest
½ cup shredded carrot

½ cup crushed pineapple, drained
½ cup flaked coconut

For the frosting
½ cup (1 stick) sweet butter,
    softened
2½ cups confectioners' sugar, sifted
2 tbsp. freshly squeezed
    orange juice
2 tbsp. orange marmalade

TIP

Lime marmalade with lime juice can replace the orange ingredients in the frosting for a really zesty alternative.

Preheat the oven to 350°F (175°C). Place 12 baking cups in a muffin pan.

In a medium bowl, sift the flour, baking powder, and cinnamon. In a large bowl cream the sugar and oil with an electric mixer until light and fluffy. Beat in the eggs slowly, then stir in the dry ingredients in 3 batches. Add the rest of the ingredients, and stir until combined. Spoon the batter into the cups. Bake for 25 minutes. Remove pan from the oven and cool for 5 minutes. Then remove the cupcakes and cool on a rack.

To make the frosting, beat the butter in a medium bowl. Add the remaining ingredients. Smear the frosting onto the cupcakes, then scatter over the remaining chopped nuts.

Store unfrosted in an airtight container for up to 3 days, or freeze for up to 3 months.

Makes 1 dozen

Hazelnut & Orange Cupcakes

For adults only! These cupcakes would be ideal on a cold winter night.

For the cupcakes
1 cup (2 sticks) sweet butter, softened
1 cup superfine sugar
2 cups all-purpose flour
3 tsp. baking powder
4 large eggs
3 tbsp. finely chopped hazelnuts
2 tbsp. Cointreau

For the frosting
1 cup cream cheese, softened
1½ cups confectioners' sugar, sifted
1 tsp. orange extract
1½ tbsp. grated orange zest
2 tbsp. chopped hazelnuts

TIP

Armagnac can also be substituted for the Cointreau for a different flavor.

Preheat the oven to 350°F (175°C). Place 18 paper baking cups in muffin pans.

Combine all the cupcake ingredients except the Cointreau in a medium bowl and beat with an electric mixer until smooth and pale, about 2–3 minutes. Spoon the batter into the cups.

Bake for 20 minutes. Remove pans from the oven and cool for 5 minutes. Pierce some holes in the tops of the cupcakes with a skewer and drizzle a little Cointreau over each. Then remove the cupcakes and cool on a rack.

To make the frosting, beat the cream cheese in a bowl with an electric mixer until light and fluffy. Beat in the confectioners' sugar for 1–2 minutes, then beat in the orange extract and zest until smooth and light. Spread the frosting on the cupcakes, then scatter over the chopped hazelnuts.

Store unfrosted for up to 2 days in an airtight container, or freeze for up to 3 months.

Makes 1½ dozen

Honey & Pine Nut Cupcakes

Sweet, dense, and stickily chewy, this simple cake is fabulous at any time of day. You could even serve it warm for dessert with whipped cream or vanilla ice cream.

For the cupcakes
1 cup (2 sticks) sweet butter, diced
½ cup clear honey
⅓ cup light corn syrup
½ cup light brown sugar
3 extra-large eggs
⅔ cup toasted pine nuts
2 cups all-purpose flour
3 tsp. baking powder

For the topping
¼ cup toasted pine nuts
4 tbsp. clear honey

Preheat the oven to 325°F (160°C). Line two 12-cup muffin pans with paper baking cups.

Put the butter, honey, corn syrup, and brown sugar in a saucepan. Heat gently over low heat, stirring, until the butter has melted and the mixture is thoroughly combined. Set aside to cool for about 10 minutes. Beat in the eggs, one at a time. Reserve 2 tablespoons of the pine nuts and stir the rest into the mixture. Sift the flour and baking powder over the mixture, then stir to combine.

Divide the mixture between the cups. Sprinkle the reserved pine nuts on top. Bake for 20 minutes until well risen and golden brown. Remove from the oven and cool for 5 minutes. Transfer to a wire rack to cool completely.

While the cupcakes are warm, prepare the topping. Put the pine nuts and honey in a pan and warm gently until runny. Drizzle over the cupcakes, spreading the mixture evenly over the top. Consume within 3 days.

Makes 2 dozen

Fruit & Nut Cupcakes

The zesty orange flavor of the frosting, together with the selection of nutty ingredients in the cupcake creates an exciting combination.

For the cupcakes
1 cup (2 sticks) sweet butter, softened
1 cup superfine sugar
2 cups all-purpose flour
3 tsp. baking powder
4 large eggs
1 tsp. orange extract
¼ cup (2 oz) raisins
¼ cup (2 oz) Brazil nuts

For the frosting
2 cups confectioners' sugar, sifted
½ cup (1 stick) sweet butter, softened
¼ cup sour cream
1 tbsp. finely grated orange zest

TIP

Add 2 tablespoons Kahlua to the frosting mix for a orange-and-Kahlua flavored delight.

Preheat the oven to 350˚F (175˚C). Place 18 paper baking cups in muffin pans.

Combine all the cupcake ingredients except the raisins and Brazil nuts in a medium bowl and beat with an electric mixer until smooth and pale, about 2–3 minutes. Stir in the raisins and Brazil nuts, then spoon the batter into the cups. Bake for 20 minutes. Remove pans from the oven and cool for 5 minutes. Then remove the cupcakes and cool on a rack.

To make the frosting, beat the confectioners' sugar and butter in a small bowl until soft and creamy. Beat in the sour cream and orange zest. Swirl onto the cooled cupcakes.

Store unfrosted in an airtight container for up to 2 days, or freeze for up to 3 months.

Makes 1½ **dozen**

Choc Chip & Walnut Cupcakes

The coffee and walnut flavors set off the sweetness of these delicious cupcakes.

For the cupcakes
1 cup (2 sticks) sweet butter, softened
1 cup superfine sugar
1¾ cups all-purpose flour
¼ cup cornflour
2½ tsp. baking powder
4 large eggs
1 tsp. vanilla extract

½ cup (3½ oz.) chopped walnuts
¼ cup (2 oz.) semisweet chocolate chips

For the frosting
1 cup (2 sticks) sweet butter, softened
3 cups confectioners' sugar, sifted
1 tbsp. instant coffee granules
1 tsp. hot coffee
1 tsp. coffee liqueur
1 tsp. vanilla extract

TIP

If you find the frosting a little too strong, replace the coffee granules with cocoa powder.

Preheat the oven to 350°F (175°C). Place 18 paper baking cups in muffin pans.

Combine all the cupcake ingredients, except the walnuts and chocolate chips, in a medium bowl and beat with an electric mixer until smooth and pale, about 2–3 minutes. Stir in the walnuts and chocolate chips. Spoon the batter into the cups. Bake for 20 minutes. Remove pans from the oven and cool for 5 minutes. Then remove the cupcakes and cool on a rack.

For the frosting, beat the butter and confectioners' sugar in a bowl until soft and creamy. Combine the coffee granules and the hot coffee, then stir into the batter. Stir in the coffee liqueur and the vanilla. Spread the frosting onto the cooled cupcakes.

Store unfrosted for up to 2 days in an airtight container, or freeze for up to 3 months.

Makes 1½ dozen

Chocolate Hazelnut & Fig Cupcakes

The combination of bittersweet chocolate and figs makes this cupcake pure decadence.

For the cupcakes
1 cup (2 sticks) sweet butter, softened
1 cup superfine sugar
1¾ cups all-purpose flour
¼ cup cornflour
2½ tsp. baking powder
4 large eggs
1 tsp. vanilla extract
½ cup (4 oz) bittersweet chocolate chips
¼ cup chopped dried figs
¼ cup finely chopped toasted hazelnuts

For the frosting
1½ cups confectioners' sugar, sifted
½ cup (1 stick) sweet butter, softened
¾ cup Dutch-process cocoa powder
2 tbsp. chocolate liqueur
1 tsp. vanilla extract

TIP

Replace the figs with the same amount of prunes for a denser cupcake texture.

Preheat the oven to 350˚F (175˚C). Place 18 paper baking cups in muffin pans.

Combine all the cupcake ingredients, except the chocolate chips, figs, and hazelnuts, in a large bowl and beat with an electric mixer until smooth and pale, about 2–3 minutes. Stir in the chocolate, figs, and hazelnuts. Spoon the batter into the cups. Bake in the oven for 20 minutes. Remove pans from the oven and cool for 5 minutes. Then remove the cupcakes and cool on a rack.

For the frosting, beat the confectioners' sugar and butter in a small bowl until creamy and smooth. Beat in the cocoa. Fold in the chocolate liqueur and vanilla. Spread the frosting onto the cooled cupcakes.

Store unfrosted in an airtight container for up to 3 days, or freeze for up to 3 months.

Makes 1½ **dozen**

Nutty Chocolate Mud Cupcakes

These cupcakes are so simple to make. Don't limit yourself to one batch.

1 cup (7 oz) semisweet
  chocolate chips
1⅓ cups (2½ sticks) sweet butter
5 large eggs
⅔ cup superfine sugar
¾ cup all-purpose flour

1 tsp. baking powder
½ cup (3½ oz) mixed nuts,
  chopped
2 tbsp. Dutch-process cocoa
  powder, for dusting

TIP

Serve with one walnut pushed into the center of each cupcake before baking, for a decorative effect.

Preheat the oven to 325°F (160°C). Place 12 paper baking cups in a muffin pan.

In a double boiler, or a medium bowl set over a pan of gently simmering water, melt the chocolate and butter together, stirring well. Let cool.

Beat the eggs and sugar in a large bowl until pale and thick. Fold the flour into the egg mixture and then stir in the melted chocolate and butter until well blended. Stir in the mixed nuts.

Spoon the mixture into the cups and bake for 20 minutes. The cupcakes will be soft and gooey in texture and appearance. Remove pan from the oven and cool for 5 minutes. Then remove the cupcakes from pan. Serve swiftly, dusted with cocoa powder.

Store in the refrigerator in an airtight container for up to 3 days, or freeze for up to 3 months.

Makes 1 dozen

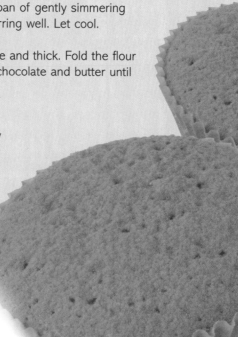

White Chocolate & Pistachio Cupcakes

Technically, white chocolate is not a chocolate, but it tastes just as decadent!

For the cupcakes
1 cup (2 sticks) sweet butter, softened
1 cup superfine sugar
1¾ cups all-purpose flour
¼ cup cornflour
2½ tsp. baking powder
4 large eggs
1 tsp. vanilla extract
½ cup (3½ oz) white chocolate chips

For the frosting
1 cup (7 oz) white chocolate chips
5 tbsp. milk
1½ cups confectioners' sugar, sifted
3 tbsp. chopped, toasted pistachio nuts

TIP

Macadamia nuts also work well, and give a creamier flavor than pistachios.

Preheat the oven to 350˚F (175˚C). Place 18 paper baking cups in muffin pans.

Combine all the cupcake ingredients, except the chocolate chips, in a large bowl and beat with an electric mixer until smooth and pale, about 2–3 minutes. Stir in the chocolate chips. Spoon the batter into the cups. Bake for 20 minutes. Remove pans from the oven and cool for 5 minutes. Then remove the cupcakes and cool on a rack.

To make the frosting, melt the chocolate and milk in a double boiler, stirring frequently. Remove from the heat and beat in the confectioners' sugar until smooth. Spread over the cupcakes and sprinkle with the nuts.

Store in an airtight container for up to 2 days, or freeze unfrosted for up to 3 months.

Makes 1½ dozen

The Fruity Ones

Fresh, dried, and frozen fruits are used to
make an enticing array of fruity-flavored
and decorated cupcakes.

The Fruity Ones

Fruity cupcakes are favorites the world over. Kids and adults alike love the naturally sweet ingredients, and these recipes are delicious no matter the season. Whether you're fond of berries, citrus, or tropical fruit, there's a fruit cupcake for everyone. The flavors will change depending on the preparation of your fruit: is it fresh? Dried? Frozen? Is it in the batter or on top of the cupcake? There are endless possibilities.

You can substitute different fruit preparations in your recipe, but be careful about levels of liquid. Very Cherry Cupcakes are delicious with fresh cherries (if they're in season) because the cherries go in the frosting rather than the batter. Similarly, Oaty Apple Cupcakes need the applesauce to make them moist; using dried apples in this recipe would be a disaster. If a recipe specifically calls for dried fruit, you can experiment with different kinds; California raisins work well in place of golden raisins, crystallized ginger can substitute for candied orange, and dried apricots or even sweet nuts like pecans can replace chopped dates.

If it's the frosting you want to change, there are some simple additions that make a big difference. For a subtly fruity flavor, make a simple white frosting and add a few drops of lemon juice or orange liqueur for "oomph." Your fruity cupcakes will be the talk of the town!

Bittersweet Citrus Cupcakes

Make these sticky cupcakes ahead of time to let the syrup soak through to the cupcake.

For the cupcakes
2 medium, seedless sweet oranges, peeled and roughly chopped
2 tbsp. grapefruit juice
½ cup (1 stick) sweet butter
1 cup superfine sugar
2 extra-large eggs
½ cup semolina
½ cup ground almond

½ cup all-purpose flour
¾ tsp. baking powder

For the syrup
1 peeled orange rind
½ peeled grapefruit rind
½ cup superfine sugar
1 cup water

TIP
This Spanish-style cupcake recipe also suits a simple lemon frosting (see page 29).

Preheat the oven to 325°F (160°C). Place 12 paper baking cups in a muffin pan.

In a saucepan, cover the oranges with water. Simmer until tender, about 15 minutes. Cool. Drain the oranges and purée in a food processor. Add the tablespoons grapefruit juice to the orange purée. In a bowl, beat the butter and sugar with an electric mixer until light.

Slowly beat in the eggs. Stir in the rest of the ingredients, along with the orange purée, until well combined. Spoon the mixture into the cups. Bake for 35 minutes. Remove pan from the oven and cool.

To make the syrup, thinly slice the orange rind, removing the pith. Do the same with the grapefruit rind. In a pan, bring the sugar and water to a simmer, stirring to dissolve the sugar. Add the orange and grapefruit strips and boil uncovered for 5 minutes, or until tender. Spoon the syrup onto each cupcake.

Store in an airtight container for up to 2 days, or freeze for up to 3 months.

Makes 1 dozen

Very Cherry Cupcakes

Fresh cherries give these cupcakes a wonderful rich flavor.

For the cupcakes
1 cup (2 sticks) sweet butter, softened
1 cup superfine sugar
2 cups all-purpose flour
3 tsp. baking powder
4 large eggs
2 tbsp. kirsch

For the frosting
3 cups confectioners' sugar, sifted
1 cup (2 sticks) sweet butter
pinch of salt
red food coloring
12 fresh cherries, stemmed

TIP
If it is hard to find fresh cherries, morello or maraschino cherries are always a favorite.

Preheat the oven to 350°F (175°C). Place 18 paper baking cups in muffin pans.

Combine all the cupcake ingredients in a large bowl and beat with an electric mixer until smooth, about 2–3 minutes. Spoon the batter into the cups. Bake for 20 minutes. Remove pans from the oven and cool for 5 minutes. Then remove the cupcakes and cool on a rack.

To make the frosting, beat the confectioners' sugar, butter, and salt in a medium bowl with an electric mixer until smooth. Add a few drops of the food coloring and beat until well combined and pink. Spread the frosting onto the cooled cupcakes and decorate with a cherry.

Store unfrosted in an airtight container for up to 3 days, or freeze for up to 3 months.

Makes 1½ dozen

Raspberry & Cottage Cheese Cupcakes

These muffins make a delicious treat whether you are counting fat grams or not!

2⅓ cups all-purpose flour
¾ cup superfine sugar
1 tbsp. baking powder
pinch of salt
2 lightly beaten extra-large eggs

4 tbsp. sunflower oil
1¼ cups low-fat milk
½ cup low-fat cottage cheese
2 cups fresh raspberries

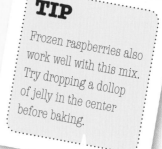

TIP

Frozen raspberries also work well with this mix. Try dropping a dollop of jelly in the center before baking.

Preheat the oven to 350˚F (175˚C). Place 12 paper baking cups in a muffin pan.

In a medium bowl, mix the flour, sugar, baking powder, and salt with a spoon.

In a large bowl, beat the eggs, oil, milk, and cottage cheese with an electric mixer until smooth. Add the flour mixure and stir until nearly combined. Fold in the raspberries, but do not over-mix. Spoon the mixture into prepared pan. Bake in the oven for 20 minutes.

Remove pan from the oven and cool for 5 minutes. Then remove the muffins and cool on a rack. Store in an airtight container for up to 2 days, or freeze for up to 3 months.

Makes 1 dozen

Oaty Apple Cupcakes

Simple to make and low in fat, this recipe is based on the classic streusel cake.

For the cupcakes
½ cup (1 stick) sweet butter, softened
¾ cup packed light brown sugar
1 lightly beaten extra-large egg
¾ cup unsweetened applesauce
2 cups all-purpose flour
3 tsp. baking powder
1 tsp. ground ginger
¼ tsp. ground cloves

For the topping
2 tbsp. butter, softened
¼ cup confectioners' sugar, sifted
3 tbsp. chopped walnuts
2 tbsp. rolled oats
2 tbsp. all-purpose flour
½ tsp. cinnamon

TIP
Add 4 tablespoons dried cranberries after adding the dry ingredients.

Preheat the oven to 350°F (175°C). Place 12 paper baking cups in a muffin pan.

In a medium bowl, beat the butter and sugar with an electric mixer until pale and creamy. Slowly add the egg and then the applesauce, beating well after each addition. Add the flour, baking powder, and spices, mixing until just combined.

To make the topping, combine all the ingredients in a small bowl. Mix with a fork until the topping resembles coarse breadcrumbs. Set aside. Spoon the batter into the cups. Sprinkle some topping on each cupcake and bake for 20–25 minutes. Remove pan from the oven and cool for 5 minutes. Then remove the cupcakes and cool on a rack.

Store in an airtight container for up to 3 days, or freeze for up to 3 months.

Makes 1 dozen

Poppy Seed & Blueberry Cupcakes

The blueberries, together with the lime zest, create a wonderfully fruity flavor to the light poppy seed batter.

For the cupcakes
1 cup (2 sticks) sweet butter, softened
1 cup superfine sugar
2 cups all-purpose flour
3 tsp. baking powder
4 large eggs
½ cup blueberries
1 tsp. vanilla extract

1 tbsp. poppy seeds
1 tbsp. grated lime zest

For the drizzle
1 cup confectioners' sugar
3 tbsp. lime juice
2 tbsp. poppy seeds
blueberries, to decorate

TIP
Replace the lime zest with lemon zest in this recipe for a similar effect.

Preheat the oven to 350°F (175°C). Place 18 paper baking cups in muffin pans.

Combine the butter, sugar, flour, baking powder, and eggs in a large bowl and beat with an electric mixer until smooth, about 2–3 minutes. Stir in the blueberries, vanilla, poppy seeds, and lime zest until well combined. Spoon the batter into the cups. Bake for 20 minutes. Remove pans from the oven and cool for 5 minutes. Then remove the cupcakes and cool on a rack.

To make the drizzle, sift the confectioners' sugar into a bowl and stir in the lime juice until it resembles the consistency of heavy cream. Stir in the poppy seeds and drizzle over the cupcakes. Decorate with blueberries.

Store in an airtight container for up to 2 days, or freeze for up to 3 months.

Makes 1½ dozen

Super Fruity Cupcakes

This recipe is a real all-rounder—a fruity meal in a cupcake!

½ cup light vegetable oil
½ cup packed brown sugar
1 lightly beaten extra-large egg
3 extra-large egg whites
1 cup shredded carrots
1 cup shredded cooking apples
1 cup raisins

½ cup chopped dates
½ cup mixed dried berries
½ cup chopped walnuts
1 tsp. allspice
4 tsp. baking powder
2¾ cups all-purpose whole
  wheat flour

TIP

Use the freshest eggs when baking— they are much easier to separate.

Preheat the oven to 350˚F (175˚C). Place 12 paper baking cups in a muffin pan.

In a large bowl, combine the oil and sugar, and beat with an electric mixer until light and smooth, about 2–3 minutes. Beat the egg and egg whites, one at a time, and then add the carrot, apple, dried fruits, and walnuts. Sift the rest of the ingredients into a medium mixing bowl. Add them to the carrot mixture, stirring until just combined.

Spoon the mixture into the cups. Bake for 20 minutes. Remove pan from the oven and cool for 5 minutes. Then remove the cupcakes and cool on a rack. Serve with a low-fat margarine spread.

Store in an airtight container for up to 3 days, or freeze for up to 3 months.

Makes 1 dozen

Chocolate & Raspberry Cupcakes

This glistening chocolate ganache is wonderful with raspberries.

For the cupcakes
½ cup fresh or thawed frozen
   raspberries
3 tbsp. water
1 cup superfine sugar
1 cup all-purpose flour
1½ tsp. baking powder
½ cup soft margarine
2 extra-large eggs
4 tbsp. Dutch-process cocoa powder

For the ganache
¾ cup (5 oz) bittersweet
   chocolate, broken
¾ cup heavy cream
12 raspberries

TIP
You could try using the same amount of blackberries instead of raspberries.

Preheat the oven to 350°F (175°C). Line a 12-cup mini muffin pan with paper baking cups.

Combine the raspberries, water, and ½ cup sugar in a small saucepan over low heat. Simmer for about 5 minutes, until the fruit starts to release its juices. Set aside to cool.

Combine the rest of the ingredients in a medium bowl and beat with an electric mixer until pale and creamy, about 2–3 minutes. Spoon the batter into the cups. Spoon a little of the fruit on top. Bake for 20 minutes. Remove the pan and cool for 5 minutes. Then remove the cupcakes and cool on a rack.

To make the ganache, melt the chocolate and cream in a double boiler over low heat, until glossy and smooth. Dollop a spoonful of ganache onto each cooled cupcake and top with a raspberry. Refrigerate until set.

Store in an airtight container for up to 2 days, or freeze without ganache for up to 3 months.

Makes 1 dozen

White Chocolate & Raspberry Cupcakes

Simple yet sophisticated—and perfect for a summer picnic!

For the cupcakes
¾ cup frozen raspberries, thawed
    (juice reserved)
1 cup (2 sticks) sweet butter,
    softened
1 cup superfine sugar
2 cups all-purpose flour
3 tsp. baking powder
4 large eggs
½ cup (3½ oz) white chocolate
    chips

For the frosting
1 cup cream cheese, softened
1½ cups confectioners' sugar, sifted
1 tsp. vanilla extract
3 tbsp. sweet butter, softened

TIP

Try replacing the cream cheese with mascarpone.

Preheat the oven to 350˚F (175˚C). Place 18 paper baking cups in muffin pans.

Thaw the raspberries by straining in a sieve, reserving the juice in a bowl below. When thawed, combine the butter, sugar, flour, baking powder, and eggs in a medium bowl. Beat with an electric mixer until light and creamy, about 2–3 minutes.

Stir in the chocolate chips, 1 tablespoon raspberry juice, and 2 tablespoons raspberries. Spoon the batter into the cups. Bake for 20 minutes. Remove pans from the oven and cool for 5 minutes. Then remove the cupcakes and cool on a rack.

To make the frosting, beat the cream cheese, confectioners' sugar, vanilla, and butter until smooth and creamy. Stir in the remaining raspberries. Spread frosting on top of the cupcakes.

Store unfrosted in an airtight container for up to 2 days, or freeze for up to 3 months.

Makes 1½ dozen

Cape Gooseberry & Orange Cupcakes

These little beauties are wonderfully tart and sweet at the same time.

For the cupcakes
1 cup (2 sticks) sweet butter, softened
1 cup superfine sugar
2 cups all-purpose flour
3 tsp. baking powder
4 large eggs
1 tbsp. vanilla extract
1 cup (5 oz) finely chopped Cape gooseberries

For the frosting
1 cup cream cheese, softened
1½ cups confectioners' sugar, sifted
1 tsp. vanilla extract
1 tbsp. grated orange zest
18 Cape gooseberries, leaves and stems attached, to decorate

TIP
Cape gooseberries are also known as golden berries, husk tomatoes, ground cherries, physalis, and poha.

Preheat the oven to 350°F (175°C). Place 18 baking cups in muffin pans.

Combine all the cupcake ingredients except the Cape gooseberries in a large bowl and beat with an electric mixer until smooth and pale, about 2–3 minutes. Add the Cape gooseberries, then spoon the batter into the cups. Bake for 20 minutes. Remove pans from the oven and cool for 5 minutes. Then remove the cupcakes and cool on a rack.

To make the frosting, beat the cream cheese, confectioners' sugar, vanilla, and orange zest with an electric mixer until soft and creamy. Smear the cupcakes with the frosting. Decorate each cake with a Cape gooseberry.

Store unfrosted in an airtight container for up to 2 days, or freeze for up to 3 months.

Makes 1½ **dozen**

Kiwi Cupcakes

Serve these cupcakes for breakfast with a glass of freshly squeezed juice.

For the cupcakes
1 cup (2 sticks) sweet butter, softened
1 cup superfine sugar
2 cups all-purpose flour
3 tsp. baking powder
4 large eggs
1 tsp. vanilla extract

For the frosting
3 cups confectioners' sugar, sifted
1 cup (2 sticks) sweet butter, softened
pinch of salt
18 thin slices kiwi fruit

TIP
For a Parisian touch, use whipping cream as a frosting and place the kiwi fruit slices on top.

Preheat the oven to 350˚F (175˚C). Place 18 paper baking cups in muffin pans.

Combine all the cupcake ingredients in a large bowl and beat with an electric mixer until smooth and pale, about 2–3 minutes. Spoon the batter into the cups. Bake for 20 minutes. Remove pans from the oven and cool for 5 minutes. Then remove the cupcakes and cool on a rack.

To make the frosting, put the confectioners' sugar, butter, and salt in a large bowl and beat with an electric mixer until smooth. Liberally spread the frosting onto the cooled cupcakes and garnish each cupcake with a slice of kiwi fruit.

Store unfrosted in an airtight container for up to 3 days, or freeze for up to 3 months.

Makes 1½ **dozen**

Banana & Raisin Cheesecake Cupcakes

Ricotta cheese is lower in fat than cream cheese and it has a great texture. A frosting with a cream cheese and orange zest flavor would work well with these cupcakes.

TIP

If you fancy a more indulgent cupcake, cream cheese can replace the ricotta.

1 cup graham cracker crumbs
3 tbsp. butter, melted
2 tbsp. honey
3 cups part-skim ricotta cheese
4 large eggs
1½ cups confectioners' sugar, sifted

¾ cup (about 2 medium) mashed bananas
1 tsp. orange extract
½ cup walnut halves
½ cup raisins

Preheat the oven to 350°F (175°C). Place 18 paper baking cups in muffin pans.

Combine all the cupcake ingredients except the Cointreau in a medium bowl and beat with an electric mixer until smooth and pale, about 2 to 3 minutes. Spoon the batter into the cups.

Bake for 20 minutes. Remove pans from the oven and cool for 5 minutes. Pierce some holes in the tops of the cupcakes with a skewer and drizzle a little Cointreau over each. Then remove the cupcakes and cool on a rack.

Store or up to 2 days in an airtight container, or freeze for up to 3 months.

Makes 1 dozen

Healthy Banana Cupcakes

These are great for a breakfast treat. They are quick to make but taste even better overnight—another reason not to be late in the morning!

½ cup finely chopped fresh banana
1¼ cups granola
2¼ cups all-purpose flour
3 tsp. baking powder
½ cup orange juice

3 tbsp. vegetable oil
¾ cup honey
1 lightly beaten extra-large egg
½ cup golden raisins

TIP

These can easily be adapted to muffins. Use a muffin pan and 2 tablespoons vegetable oil instead of 3 to make this adaptation.

Preheat the oven to 350°F (175°C). Place 12 paper baking cups in a muffin pan.

Mix the banana, granola, flour, and baking powder in a medium bowl with a spoon. Set aside. Beat the orange juice, oil, honey, and egg in a large bowl with an electric mixer. Add the flour mixture to the egg mixture, and stir until just combined. Fold in the golden raisins.

Spoon the mixture into the prepared pan. Bake for 20 minutes. Remove pan from the oven and cool for 5 minutes. Then remove the cupcakes and cool on a rack.

Store in an airtight container for up to 3 days, or freeze for up to 3 months.

Makes 1 dozen

Orange Zest Cupcakes

Candied oranges are a lovely presentation choice—they suit these orange-flavored delights perfectly.

For the cupcakes
1 cup (2 sticks) sweet butter, softened
1 cup superfine sugar
2 cups all-purpose flour
3 tsp. baking powder
4 large eggs
1 tbsp. finely grated orange zest

For the frosting
1 cup cream cheese, softened
1½ cups confectioners' sugar, sifted
1 tsp. orange extract
18 candied orange segments, to decorate

TIP

Lightly crushed fennel seeds add an exciting twist to these cupcakes.

Preheat the oven to 350°F (175°C). Place 18 paper baking cups in muffin pans.

Combine all the cupcake ingredients in a medium bowl and beat with an electric mixer until smooth and pale, about 2–3 minutes. Spoon the batter into the cups. Bake for 20 minutes. Remove pans from the oven and cool for 5 minutes. Then remove the cupcakes and cool on a rack.

To make the frosting, combine the cream cheese and confectioners' sugar, and beat briskly until soft and creamy. Add the orange extract and stir well. Swirl onto the top of the cupcakes, and decorate with the candied orange segments.

Store unfrosted for up to 3 days in an airtight container, or freeze for 3 months.

Makes 1½ **dozen**

Strawberry & Balsamic Cupcakes

A picnic favorite for the summer months, these have a sweet but sophisticated flavor.

For the cupcakes
1 cup (2 sticks) sweet butter, softened
1 cup superfine sugar
2 cups all-purpose flour
3 tsp. baking powder
4 large eggs
1 tsp. strawberry extract

For the frosting
1 cup cream cheese, softened
1½ cups confectioners' sugar, sifted
2 tsp. sweet balsamic vinegar
3 tbsp. sweet butter, softened
3 tbsp. chopped fresh strawberries
18 slices strawberries, to decorate

TIP

Squeeze a little lemon juice onto the strawberries to make sure they do not lose their freshness.

Preheat the oven to 350°F (175°C). Place 18 paper baking cups in muffin pans.

Combine the butter, sugar, flour, baking powder, eggs, and strawberry extract in a medium bowl. Beat with an electric mixer until light and creamy, about 2–3 minutes. Spoon the batter into the cups. Bake for 20 minutes. Remove pans from the oven and cool for 5 minutes. Then remove the cupcakes and cool on a rack.

To make the frosting, beat the cream cheese, confectioners' sugar, balsamic vinegar, and butter until smooth and creamy. Stir in the chopped strawberries. Spread frosting on top of the cupcakes and decorate with strawberry slices.

Store unfrosted in an airtight container for up to 2 days, or freeze for up to 3 months.

Makes 1½ **dozen**

Fruity Madeira Cupcakes

Sometimes the simplest cupcakes are the best, and this plain, golden, lemony cupcake is no exception, especially with a new addition of raisins.

2 sticks butter, at room temperature
    generous ¾ cup superfine sugar,
plus 1–2 tbsp. for sprinkling
3 extra-large eggs
¾ cup golden raisins

2 cups all-purpose flour
1½ tsp. baking powder
finely grated zest and juice
    of 1 lemon

TIP

These are delicious with a cup of tea or coffee.

Preheat the oven to 325°F (160°C). Place 18 paper baking cups in muffin pans.

Beat together the butter and sugar until pale and creamy, then beat in the eggs one at a time. Stir in the raisins. Sift the flour over the mixture, then fold it in. Fold in the lemon zest and juice.

Spoon the batter into the cups, smoothing the top with the back of the spoon. Sprinkle the tops with 1–2 tablespoons sugar and bake for about 20 minutes until golden and risen.

Let the cupcakes cool in the pans for about 10 minutes. Then remove the cupcakes and cool on a rack.

Store in an airtight container for up to 3 days, or freeze for up to 3 months.

Makes 1½ **dozen**

Fruity Lemon Drizzle Cupcakes

These cupcakes are utterly simple to make.

For the cupcakes
½ cup (1 stick) plus 1 tbsp. butter, at room temperature
⅔ cup superfine sugar
2 extra-large eggs
finely grated zest of 1 lemon
½ cup mixed dried cherries and blueberries

1 cup all-purpose flour
1½ tsp. baking soda

For the topping
6 tbsp. superfine sugar
juice of 1 lemon, plus strips of the zest

TIP

The intense lemony flavor comes from drenching the tender golden cakes with lemon syrup while they're still warm—so make sure you do it straight away!

Preheat the oven to 350°F (175°C). Place 18 paper baking cups in muffin pans.

Beat together the butter and sugar until pale and creamy. Beat in the eggs, one at a time, then stir in the lemon zest. Stir in the dried cherries and blueberries. Sift the flour and baking powder over the mixture, then fold in. Spoon the mixture into the cups and smooth out evenly. Bake for about 15 minutes until risen and golden.

Place the cups on a cooling rack. Prick the top of the cupcakes with a skewer.

Combine the sugar and lemon juice and immediately drizzle over the top of the cupcakes. Let the cakes cool in the pans. Store in an airtight container for up to 2 days, or freeze for up to 3 months.

Makes 1½ **dozen**

Orange, Apricot & Hazelnut Cupcakes

Sweet, nutty, and rich with the intense flavor of apricot, these cupcakes are perfect for any occasion. Bake them when you have guests for coffee, or just enjoy them as an everyday treat.

⅔ cup roasted hazelnuts
1½ sticks sweet butter, at room temperature
½ cup superfine sugar
¼ cup light brown sugar
2 extra-large eggs

finely grated zest of 1 orange
scant 1¼ cups all-purpose flour
1½ tsp. baking powder
⅔ cup dried apricots, chopped

TIP

Soak the apricots in corn syrup for a really sweet flavor.

Preheat the oven to 350°F (175°C). Place 12 paper baking cups in muffin pans.

Put the hazelnuts in a food processor and process until coarsely ground, then set aside.

Beat together the butter and sugars until smooth and creamy, then beat in the eggs one at a time. Stir in the orange zest, then sift the flour and baking powder over the batter. Add the ground nuts and fold together until well mixed. Fold in the apricots.

Spoon the mixture into the cups, smoothing out the top with the back of the spoon. Bake for 20–25 minutes until golden and risen. Remove pans from the oven and cool for 5 minutes. Then remove the cupcakes and cool on a rack.

Makes 1 dozen

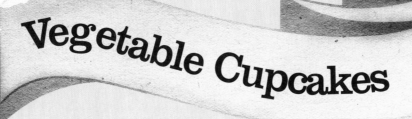

Vegetable Cupcakes

Unlikely as it may sound, some vegetables can be used to make great cakes—just think of the classic carrot cake. Then it's just a small step to Zucchini & Feta, Red Bell Pepper & Cheddar, and Pumpkin & Ginger.

Vegetable Cupcakes

Vegetable cupcakes are among the most delicious varieties. Many people overlook the charms of these savory treats, but the flavor combinations are endless, low-fat, full of vitamins, and satisfy hunger pangs like no other type of cupcake. These recipes can be a little labor-intensive, so a few simple hints and tips can speed things along beautifully.

Unless you have all the right kitchen gadgets, shredding and grating vegetables is very time consuming. Your cupcakes will fall apart if the chunks of vegetables are too big, but a flat grater with sliding hand protector speeds things along. Alternatively, chop finely or pulse in a food processor. Similarly, hard cheeses like Cheddar will need to be quite fine; you can buy these ready-grated from the fresh aisle in the supermarket.

These cupcakes do not lend themselves to sweet and sugary frostings, but rich and creamy toppings made with fresh soft cheese like mascarpone, are both mouthwatering and filling. To top things off, pumpkin, carrot, and beet flavors go particularly well with a little honey, so serve with coffee in the afternoon for a perfect snack.

Caramelized Onion Cupcakes

These savory delights are great with cheese, pickle, and a picnic spread.

2 tbsp. olive oil
1 lb. (about 3) finely sliced medium onions
1 tsp. dried crushed chilies
4 cups all-purpose flour
2¼ cups cornmeal
1 tbsp. baking powder
pinch of salt
2 lightly beaten extra-large eggs

1½ (3 sticks) cups sweet butter, melted
1⅓ cups buttermilk
1 tbsp. chopped fresh thyme leaves

TIP

You could try Vidalia onions, which have an incredible natural sweetness.

Heat the oil in a medium skillet. Add the onions and cook over medium heat, stirring occasionally until they are soft and caramelized, about 15 minutes. Set aside to cool.

Preheat the oven to 350˚F (175˚C). Place 12 paper baking cups in a muffin pan.

In a medium bowl, mix the chilies, flour, cornmeal, baking powder, and salt with a spoon. In a large bowl, beat the eggs, butter, buttermilk, and thyme until combined. Stir in half the cooked onions. Stir in the flour mixture until just combined. Spoon the mixture into the cups. Top with the remaining cooked onions. Bake for 20 minutes.

Remove pan from the oven and cool for 5 minutes. Then remove the cupcakes and serve warm.

Store refrigerated in an airtight container for up to 2 days, or freeze for up to 3 months.

Makes 1 dozen

Carrot & Cashew Nut Cupcakes

Carrot cake somehow doesn't seem to be as naughty as other cakes!

For the cupcakes
1 cup (2 sticks) sweet butter, softened
1 cup superfine sugar
2 cups all-purpose flour
3 tsp. baking powder
4 large eggs
1 tsp. allspice
1 cup chopped cashew nuts
1 cup freshly shredded carrots
2 tbsp. golden raisins

For the frosting
1 cup marscarpone, softened
1½ cups confectioners' sugar, sifted
1 tbsp. lemon juice
1 tsp. vanilla extract

TIP
Leave off the frosting for a healthier recipe.

Preheat the oven to 350°F (175°C). Place 18 paper baking cups in muffin pans.

Combine the butter, sugar, flour, baking powder and eggs in a large bowl and beat with an electric mixer until smooth, about 2–3 minutes. Stir in the rest of the ingredients. Spoon the batter into the cups. Bake for 20 minutes. Remove pans from the oven and cool for 5 minutes. Then remove the cupcakes and cool on a rack.

To make the frosting, slowly beat the marscapone and confectioners' sugar in a large bowl with an electric mixer until creamy and soft. Add the lemon juice and vanilla and beat briskly until well combined. Spread the frosting liberally onto the cooled cupcakes.

Store unfrosted for up to 3 days in an airtight container, or freeze for up to 3 months.

Makes 1½ dozen

Zucchini & Feta Cupcakes

These savory cupcakes offer a flavor from the Mediterranean. You'll find zucchini and feta combined in Greek and Turkish salads, alongside plump olives and flatbreads.

TIP

Serve these with sundried tomato and olive salad.

2 cups all-purpose flour
1 tbsp. baking powder
pinch of salt
2 extra-large eggs
½ cup virgin olive oil, plus a little
    extra for greasing
1½ cups (about 2 or 3 medium)
    shredded zucchini
1 cup crumbled feta cheese
1½ tbsp. grated lemon zest

Preheat the oven to 350°F (175°C). Place
18 paper baking cups in muffin pans.

Sift the dry ingredients together in a medium bowl.
In a large bowl, beat the eggs and oil with an electric
mixer until smooth. Stir in the zucchini, feta cheese,
and lemon zest. Add the dry ingredients, and stir until
the mixture is just combined.

Spoon the mixture into the prepared cases. Bake for
30 minutes. Remove pan from the oven and cool for
5 minutes. Remove the cupcakes and cool on a rack.

Store refrigerated in an airtight container for up to 2 days,
or freeze for up to 3 months.

Makes 1½ dozen

Beet & Chocolate Cupcakes

Do not be alarmed—these cupcakes are truly marvelous! Use fresh beets, with the skin on, not canned.

1½ lb. (about 2 large) fresh
   trimmed beets
3½ cups all-purpose flour
2 tbsp. Dutch-process cocoa powder
1 cup superfine sugar
1 tbsp. baking powder
2 extra-large eggs
½ cup vegetable oil
1½ cups buttermilk

TIP

When skinning the beets, you may wish to wear latex gloves to avoid staining your hands purple!

Steam the beets for 50 minutes, until tender. Drain and rinse under cold water. When cool enough to handle, gently peel away the skin with your fingertips. Place the peeled beets in a food processor and blend until smooth. Set aside.

Preheat the oven to 350°F (175°C). Place 18 baking cups in muffin pans.

In a medium bowl, combine the flour, cocoa, sugar, and baking powder. In a large bowl, beat the eggs, oil, and buttermilk. Stir in the beets until well combined. Add the flour mixture, stirring until just combined.

Spoon the batter into the cups. Bake for 20 minutes. Remove pans from the oven and cool for 5 minutes. Then remove the cupcakes and cool on a rack.

Store in an airtight container for up to 2 days, or freeze for up to 3 months.

Makes 1½ dozen

Beet & Carrot Cupcakes

Lower in fat than a classic frosted carrot cake, these rich, sweet, dense little cakes are flecked with ruby red shreds of beet. Even if you don't like beets, you'll love these.

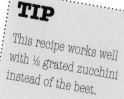

TIP

This recipe works well with ½ grated zucchini instead of the beet.

For the cupcakes
1½ cups all-purpose flour
2 tsp. baking powder
⅔ cup light brown sugar
1 tsp. ground cinnamon
½ tsp. ground ginger
1 large banana, mashed
1 medium carrot, grated
1 beet, grated (about 1½ inches in diameter)

2 extra-large eggs, beaten
⅔ cup vegetable oil

For the frosting
3½ oz cream cheese
2 tbsp. confectioners' sugar, sifted
1 tsp. finely grated lemon zest

Preheat the oven to 350°F (175°C). Place 18 paper baking cups in muffin pans.

Combine the flour, baking powder, brown sugar, and spices in a large bowl. Make a well in the center. Add the banana, carrot, beet, eggs, and oil. Stir to combine thoroughly.

Spoon the batter into the cups, and bake for about 20–25 minutes until risen and golden. Turn out onto a wire rack and let cool completely.

To make the frosting, stir together the cream cheese, sugar, and lemon zest. Swirl frosting on top of the cakes.

Store unfrosted in an airtight container for up to 2 days, or freeze for up to 3 months.

Makes 1½ dozen

Carrot & Cardamom Cupcakes

There are a great many variations of this classic cake, but these cupcakes flavored with orange, cardomom, and ginger are particularly good. The sweet, crumbly, delicious sponge cake gets better over time.

For the cupcakes
¾ cup light brown sugar
¼ cup superfine sugar
1 cup vegetable oil
3 extra-large eggs
finely grated zest of 1 orange
seeds from 8 cardamom pods,
    crushed
½ tsp. ground ginger
2 cups all-purpose flour
3 tsp. baking powder
2 large carrots, grated
    (about 2 cups)
¾ cup chopped walnuts

TIP

1 teaspoon cinnamon and 1 teaspoon apple juice also work well with the flavors in these cupcakes.

Preheat the oven to 350°F (175°C). Place 18 paper baking cups in muffin pans.

Beat together the sugars, oil, and eggs. Stir in the orange zest, crushed cardamom, and ginger. Sift the flour over the bowl, then fold in. Fold in the carrots and walnuts. Spoon the mixture into the prepared pans. Bake for 20–30 minutes until risen and golden. Turn out onto a wire rack to cool completely.

Store in an airtight container for up to 4 days, or freeze for up to 3 months.

Makes 1½ dozen

Zucchini, Lime & Pistachio Cupcakes

These cupcakes are tender and sweet with the sharp zest of lime—
they also happen to be dairy-free!

For the cupcakes
2 extra-large eggs
⅓ cup vegetable oil
½ cup superfine sugar
   seeds from 6 cardamom pods,
   crushed
½ tsp. ground ginger
1 large (about ½ lb.) zucchini,
   grated
½ cup shelled pistachio nuts,
   chopped

1⅓ cups all-purpose flour
1½ tsp. baking powder

For the syrup
finely grated zest and juice of
   2 limes
⅓ cup superfine sugar
½ cup shelled pistachio nuts,
   chopped

TIP

Add in a teaspoon
chopped and seeded
red chili to the syrup.
It adds a kick, and the
flavor really works!

Preheat the oven to 350°F (175°C). Place 18 paper baking cups
in muffin pans.

Beat together the eggs, oil, sugar, crushed cardamom, and ginger. Fold
in the grated zucchini and chopped nuts. Sift the flour and baking powder
over the bowl, then fold in. Spoon the mixture into the prepared pan,
smoothing the top with the back of the spoon.

Bake for about 20–25 minutes until risen and a skewer inserted
in the center comes out clean. Let the cakes cool in the pan for
5 minutes, then turn out onto a wire rack to cool completely.

To make the syrup, put the grated lime zest and lime juice in a pan
and add the sugar. Warm gently, stirring, until the sugar has
dissolved, then boil for 1 minute. Remove from the heat, stir in the
nuts, and let cool for 10–15 minutes to thicken. Pour the syrup over the
cake and let them stand for at least 30 minutes before serving.

Store in an airtight container for up to 4 days, or freeze for up to 3 months.

Makes 1½ **dozen**

Eggplant Caviar Cupcakes

The caviar in the title actually refers to the eggplant seeds, or "eggs."

For the cupcakes
2 small eggplants
6 tbsp. extra virgin olive oil
2½ cups all-purpose flour
3½ tsp. baking powder
pinch of salt
1 lightly beaten extra-large egg
1¼ cups milk

For the butter
½ cup (1 stick) sweet butter,
   softened
2 cloves garlic, finely minced
2 tsp. sherry vinegar
1 tbsp. chopped basil
pinch of salt and pepper

Preheat the oven to 400°F (200°C). Rub the eggplants with 2 tablespoons olive oil.

Bake on a cookie sheet for 30 minutes, until the eggplant softens and turns dark brown. When cool enough to handle, remove the tops and slice lengthwise. Using a spoon, scrape the flesh away from the skin. Discard the skin and roughly chop the eggplant flesh. Set aside.

Place 12 paper baking cups in muffin pans. In a medium bowl, combine the dry ingredients. In a large bowl, beat the egg, milk, and remaining olive oil. Mix in the flour mixture until nearly combined. Fold in the chopped eggplant. Spoon the mixture into the prepared pans. Bake for 25 minutes. Remove pan from the oven and cool for 5 minutes. Then remove the cupcakes and cool on a rack.

To make the butter, combine the butter, garlic, vinegar, and basil in a bowl. Beat until well combined, then season with salt and pepper. Spread over the top of the cupcakes or serve as an accompaniment on the side.

Store in an airtight container for up to 2 days, or freeze for up to 3 months.

Makes 1 dozen

Red Bell Pepper & Cheddar Cupcakes

These cupcakes, with delicious parsley butter, are perfect for a cold winter's day.

For the cupcakes
6 tbsp. extra virgin olive oil
2½ cups all-purpose flour
4 tsp. baking powder
pinch of salt
1 lightly beaten extra-large egg
1¼ cups milk
3 tbsp. minced red bell pepper

½ cup grated Cheddar cheese, plus
a little extra for sprinkling

For the butter
½ cup (1 stick) sweet butter,
softened
pinch of salt and pepper
1 tbsp. chopped fresh parsley

TIP

Monterey Jack cheese can be substituted if Cheddar is hard to come by.

Preheat the oven to 400°F (200°C). Place 12 paper baking cups in a muffin pan.

In a medium bowl, combine the dry ingredients. In a large bowl, beat the egg, milk, and olive oil. Mix in the flour mixture until nearly combined. Fold in the red bell pepper and cheese. Spoon the mixture into the cups, then sprinkle over remaining cheese. Bake for 25 minutes. Remove pan from the oven and cool for 5 minutes. Then remove the cupcakes and cool on a rack.

To make the butter, beat the parsley into the butter until well combined, then season with salt and pepper. Serve as an accompaniment to the cupcakes.

Store in an airtight container for up to 2 days, or freeze for up to 3 months.

Makes 1 dozen

Tomato, Thyme & Ricotta Cupcakes

Sun-dried tomatoes, thyme, and ricotta cheese combine for this wonderfully crumbly, delectable savory cupcake.

6 tbsp. extra virgin olive oil
2½ cups all-purpose flour
4 tsp. baking powder
pinch of salt
1 lightly beaten egg

1¼ cups milk
½ cup ricotta
3 tbsp. minced sun-dried tomato
1 tbsp. freshly chopped
  thyme leaves

TIP

You could use tomato paste in place of the minced sun-dried tomatoes.

Preheat the oven to 400˚F (200˚C). Place 12 paper baking cups in a muffin pan.

In a medium bowl, combine the dry ingredients. In a large bowl, beat the egg, milk, ricotta, and the olive oil. Mix in the flour mixture until nearly combined. Fold in the tomato and thyme. Spoon the mixture into the cups. Bake for 25 minutes. Remove pan from the oven and cool for 5 minutes. Then remove the cupcakes and cool on a rack.

Store in an airtight container for up to 2 days, or freeze for up to 3 months.

Makes 1 dozen

Pumpkin & Ginger Cupcakes

These cupcakes are a delicious fall treat.

2⅔ cups all-purpose flour
⅓ cup packed light brown sugar
1 tbsp. baking powder
½ tsp. nutmeg
½ tsp. ground cloves
1 tsp. ground ginger
pinch of salt

1 lightly beaten extra-large egg
½ cup puréed pumpkin, fresh
   or canned
¾ cup fat-free milk
⅓ cup sunflower oil
3 tbsp. chopped candied ginger
4 tbsp. pumpkin seeds

TIP

If you can't find fresh pumpkin, then use canned pumpkin.

Preheat the oven to 350°F (175°C). Line a 12-cup muffin pan with paper baking cups.

In a medium bowl, combine the dry ingredients with a spoon. In a large bowl, beat the egg, pumpkin, milk, and oil with an electric mixer until well combined. Add the flour mixture to the pumpkin mixture, mixing until nearly combined. Fold in the candied ginger, but do not over-mix. Spoon the batter into the cups. Sprinkle each cupcake with a few of the pumpkin seeds.

Bake for 20 minutes. Remove pan from the oven and cool for 5 minutes. Then remove the cupcakes and cool on a rack.

Store in an airtight container for up to 2 days, or freeze for up to 3 months.

Makes 1 dozen

Cheese, Tomato & Bacon Cupcakes

An alternative to the fried breakfast, this is a Saturday morning treat.

For the cupcakes
6 cups all-purpose flour
3 tsp. dried yeast
9–10 fl. oz milk
3½ fl. oz olive oil
1 tbsp. salt
1 tbsp. sugar

For the filling
5 oz dried tomatoes, in oil
4 tbsp. crème fraîche
4 tomatoes, skinned and diced
1 bunch basil, chopped
7 oz cheese, grated
flour for working

Preheat the oven to 400°F (200°C). Place 26 paper cups in muffin pans.

Combine all the cupcake ingredients (following your yeast packet instructions), and knead to a pliable dough. Cover and let rest in a warm place for about 45 minutes. Drain and chop the dried tomatoes. Knead the dough again, then roll out on a floured work surface to a rectangle measuring 30×8 in.

Spread with crème fraîche and scatter with the chopped fresh and dried tomatoes, basil and grated cheese, leaving about 1 in. free at the edges. Brush the top edge with a little water. Then roll up lengthwise into a long roll, cut into approximately 1-in. slices and place in the prepared paper cups. Bake in an oven for 15–20 minutes, until golden brown.

Store in an airtight container to up to 3 days, or freeze for up to a month.

Makes 26

Potato Cupcakes

The savory equivalent of a cherry bun, these tomato-topped delicacies are healthy and very quick to bake.

1 cup pastry flour
1 scant cup cooked, riced potatoes
½ tsp. salt
a good pinch of nutmeg
¾ cup Emmental cheese,
   finely grated

2½ tsp. baking powder
½ tsp. baking soda
1 extra-large egg
1¾ fl oz vegetable oil
1¼ buttermilk
12 cherry tomatoes

Preheat the oven to 350°F (180°C). Line a 12-cup muffin pan with paper cups.

Put the flour into a bowl and mix with the potatoes, seasonings, cheese, baking powder and baking soda.

Whisk the egg, add the vegetable oil and buttermilk and mix well. Then stir the dry ingredients into the liquid ingredients, mixing just long enough to moisten the dry ingredients.

Divide the mixture between the cups and top each with a cherry tomato. Bake for 20–30 minutes. Leave to rest in the pan for 5 minutes, then take out and serve warm.

Makes 1 dozen

Pea & Ham Cupcakes

A meal in a cupcake, these little muffin-like cakes are healthy, spicy, and delicious.

2½ cups all-purpose flour
2 tsp. baking powder
1 tsp. curry powder
pinch of ground ginger
1 extra-large egg
pinch of salt
7 fl. oz yogurt

3½ fl. oz oil
1 cup frozen peas, thawed
1 cup scallions, trimmed and
  finely diced
12 cubes cooked ham
½ cup cheese, grated

TIP

You couple replace the peas for the same amount of sweetcorn for a different flavor.

Preheat the oven to 350°F (180°C). Line the holes of a muffin pan with baking parchment.

Mix the flour, baking powder, curry powder, and ginger. Beat the egg with a pinch of salt and mix with the yogurt and oil. Quickly stir in the dry ingredients. Carefully fold in the peas and scallions with a flexible spatula.

Divide a third of the mixture between the holes, put a cube of ham in each and cover with the rest of the mixture. Sprinkle with cheese and bake in the oven for 30 minutes until golden brown.

Take out of the oven, leave to rest in the pan for 5 minutes, then carefully lift out of the pan. Cool on a cake rack.

Store in an airtight container for up to 2 days, or freeze for up to 3 months.

Makes 1 dozen

Sweetcorn & Bacon Cupcakes

These lovely little cupcakes would work nicely at a buffet-style dinner party, or served on a salad for a unusual appetizer.

1 cup all-purpose flour
pinch of salt
¼ cup sugar
1½ tsp. baking powder
¼ cup margarine
1 cup cornmeal

1 extra-large egg
1 cup milk
½–¾ cup sweetcorn kernels, canned
⅓ cup smoked bacon, finely diced

Preheat the oven to 400°F (200°C). Line a 12-cup muffin pan with paper cups.

Put the flour, salt, sugar, and baking powder into a food mixer, add the margarine and mix until the ingredients resemble fine breadcrumbs.

Add the egg and milk and mix until the dry ingredients are moist. Stir in the sweetcorn kernels and bacon. Divide the mixture between the paper cups.

Bake in the oven for 20–25 minutes. Serve hot or cold.

Makes 1 dozen

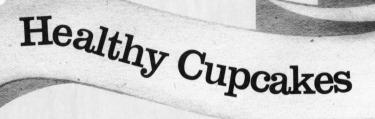

Healthy Cupcakes

You may have special dietary requirements but you don't have to miss out on eating cupcakes. This chapter offers healthy alternatives including high fiber, reduced sugar, vegan, and gluten-free options.

Healthy Cupcakes

Healthy cupcakes are guilt-free, delicious morsels of snacking heaven. If you don't have time in the morning for a big bowl of grape nuts or granola, get your fiber from a mid-morning healthy cupcake. You can treat these recipes like stand-alone snacks, or have them with lunch—spread with a little low-fat cream cheese or dipped in yogurt. Sweet or hearty, these cupcakes suit a wide range of serving suggestions.

When you need to spice up your lunch, Basil Pesto and Chili Cupcakes go especially well with tomato soup; they also add an Italian twist to traditional Boston chowder. Vegan options allow you to get that sweet fix without tipping the scales, and you avoid artificial ingredients. Be careful, once you've tried vegan chocolate recipes, you may never feel the same way about store-bought triple chocolate chip.

Allergies and intolerances can spoil cupcake fun, but dairy and gluten-free recipes widen your options and they're lower in fat and simple sugars too! Often allergy-friendly recipes just tell you to substitute soymilk or buy expensive gluten-free flour, but these scrumptious recipes achieve authentic cupcake-goodness using a range of methods. Enjoy your healthy cupcakes!

Basil Pesto & Chili Cupcakes

These unusually savory cupcakes make an ideal wholesome treat.

For the cupcakes
¾ cup yellow cornmeal
1 cup all-purpose flour
1½ tsp. baking powder
3 tbsp. sugar
pinch of salt
1 tsp. chili flakes
2 extra-large eggs
1 cup whole milk
4 tbsp. (½ stick) sweet butter,
  melted

For the frosting
½ cup basil pesto
1½ cups cream cheese, softened
12 cherry tomatoes

TIP

Arugula pesto also works very well with this recipe.

Preheat the oven to 350°F (175°C). Place 12 paper baking cups in a muffin pan.

In a medium bowl, stir the dry ingredients. Beat the eggs, milk, and butter in a large bowl with an electric mixer until combined. Add the flour mixture to the egg mixture, and stir until just combined. Spoon the batter into the cups. Bake for 20 minutes. Remove pan and cool for 5 minutes. Then remove the cupcakes and cool on a rack.

For the frosting, beat the pesto and cream cheese with an electric mixer until smooth and creamy. Smear the frosting onto the cooled cupcakes and top with the cherry tomatoes.

Store in an airtight container for up to 3 days, or freeze for up to 3 months.

Makes 1 dozen

Chocolate & Coffee Vegan Cupcakes

To make these authentically vegan you must use specially labeled vegan chocolate chips.

2 ½ cups all-purpose flour
4 tbsp. Dutch-process cocoa powder
pinch of salt
2 cups superfine sugar
½ cup unsweetened applesauce
2 cups cold water

2 tsp. white vinegar
2 tsp. baking soda
¼ cup (2 fl. oz) hot coffee
1 cup (6 oz) semisweet vegan
    chocolate chips
confectioners' sugar for dusting

TIP

Why not try making a vegan buttercream frosting to go on top? Combine tofu, lemon juice, maple syrup, and vanilla extract.

Preheat the oven to 375˚F (190˚C). Place 12 paper baking cups in a muffin pan.

Sift the flour, cocoa, salt, and sugar into a large bowl and set aside. In a separate large bowl, combine the applesauce, water, vinegar, baking soda, and hot coffee. Add the flour mixture and stir well to combine. Fold in the chocolate chips. Spoon the mixture into the cups. Bake for about 20 minutes.

Remove pan from the oven and cool for 5 minutes. Then remove the cupcakes and cool on a rack. Serve dusted with sugar.

Store in an airtight container for up to 3 days, or freeze for up to 3 months.

Makes 1 dozen

Egg-Free Choc Cupcakes

These deliciously moist, egg-free cupcakes are simple to prepare. The cherry cola lends a subtle, sweet fruitiness.

1 cup (2 sticks) sweet butter, softened
14 oz can condensed milk
2 cups all-purpose flour
1 cup Dutch-process cocoa powder
2 tsp. baking powder
½ cup (3 ½ oz) semisweet chocolate chips
1 tsp. vanilla extract
1½ cups cherry cola

TIP

Try lemonade or orangeade instead of the cherry cola for a slightly sweeter flavor.

Preheat the oven to 350˚F (175˚C). Place 12 paper baking cups in a muffin pan.

In a medium bowl, cream the butter with an electric mixer until light, about 2–3 minutes. Add the condensed milk and beat until combined. Sift the flour, cocoa, and baking powder into the wet mixture. Stir in the chocolate chips, vanilla, and cola.

Spoon the batter into the cups. Bake for 20 minutes. Remove pan from the oven and cool for 5 minutes. Then remove the cupcakes and cool on a rack.

Store in an airtight container for up to 3 days, or freeze for up to 3 months.

Makes 1 dozen

Sugar-free Prune Cupcakes

These great little cupcakes are packed full of fiber and contain no refined sweeteners.

1 cup mixed-grain cereal
2 cups boiling water
1½ cups all-purpose flour
1 tbsp. baking powder
4 tbsp. honey
pinch of salt
1 lightly beaten extra-large egg
⅓ cup safflower oil
4 tbsp. chopped dried prunes

In a medium bowl, mix the cereal and water. Set aside for 20 minutes for the grains to swell.

Preheat the oven to 400°F (200°C). Place 12 paper baking cups into a muffin pan.

In a medium bowl sift the flour and baking powder. In a large bowl, beat the honey, salt, egg, and oil. Slowly add the flour and the cereal and mix well. Stir in the prunes, then spoon the mixture into the cups. Bake in the oven for 20 minutes. Remove pan from the oven and cool for 5 minutes. Then remove the cupcakes and cool on a rack.

Store in an airtight container for up to 3 days, or freeze for up to 3 months.

Makes 1 dozen

TIP

Replace the prunes with ½ cup mashed banana for a different flavor.

Dairy-free Pear & Ginger Cupcakes

Great for anyone on a dairy-free diet, these dense, moist cakes with their delicate taste of pear and sugary, peppery bite of stem ginger make a great choice for afternoon tea.

For the cupcakes
3 extra-large eggs
⅔ cup vegetable oil
2 pears, grated
4 pieces of stem ginger in syrup, chopped
1½ cups all-purpose flour
1 tsp. baking powder
1 tsp. ground ginger

½ tsp. freshly grated nutmeg
generous ¾ cup superfine sugar

For the frosting
2 cups sifted confectioners' sugar
1 stick plus 2 tbsp. soft butter
2 tsp. lemon juice
2 tsp. ginger syrup (from a jar of stem ginger)

Preheat the oven to 350°F (175°C). Place 12 paper baking cups in a muffin pan.

Put the eggs and oil in a bowl and beat together to combine, then stir in the grated pears and stem ginger. Combine the flour, baking powder, ginger, nutmeg, and sugar, and sift over the egg mixture. Fold together until well mixed.

Pour the batter into the cups and bake for 20–30 minutes until risen and golden. Let cool in the pan for a few minutes, then transfer to a wire rack to cool completely.

For the frosting, beat all the ingredients together until smooth and creamy, then spoon over the cooled cupcakes.

Store in an airtight container for up to 3 days, or freeze for up to 3 months.

Makes 1 dozen

Crispy Creamy Cupcakes

This simple refrigerator cake is great for anyone avoiding gluten or eggs, but it's also a smashing cake for a kids' party.

For the cupcakes
9 oz milk chocolate
¼ stick butter
3¼ cups cornflakes
¾ cup Brazil nuts, roughly chopped
2½ oz mini-marshmallows (or larger marshmallows snipped into pieces)

For the frosting
3½ oz mascarpone
2 tsp. confectioners' sugar

Place 12 paper baking cups in a muffin pan.

Break the chocolate into pieces and put them in a heatproof bowl with the butter. Place the bowl over a pan of barely simmering water and let the chocolate and butter melt. Remove from the heat, stir to combine, then let cool slightly.

Meanwhile, put the cornflakes in a bag and crush lightly with a rolling pin. Combine with the nuts and marshmallows, then stir into the melted chocolate.

Divide the mixture between the cups, spreading out in an even layer to come only halfway up each cup, then chill for about 1 hour until set.

Beat the mascarpone with the sugar and spread over six cupcakes. Carefully remove the remaining six cupcakes from their cups and sandwich together with the iced cupcakes.

Store in an airtight container for up to 3 days, or freeze for up to 3 months.

Makes 1 dozen

Dairy-free Custard Cupcakes

These delicious cupcakes are topped with thick soy custard and fresh strawberries. They're the perfect alternative to traditional sponge cakes for anyone on a dairy-free diet.

For the cupcakes
4 large eggs, separated
⅔ cup superfine sugar
2 tbsp. cornstarch
2 tbsp. arrowroot
½ tsp. cream of tartar
½ tsp. baking soda
1 tbsp. light corn syrup, warmed
1 tsp. vanilla extract

For the filling
3 extra-large egg yolks
2 tbsp. superfine sugar
1 tbsp. all-purpose flour
1 cup soy milk
1 tsp. vanilla

To decorate
12 small strawberries
confectioners' sugar, for dusting

TIP
Try substituting the finely grated zest of 1 lemon for the vanilla in this recipe.

Preheat the oven to 350°F (175°C). Place 12 paper baking cups in a muffin pan.

Put the egg whites in a clean, grease-free bowl and whisk to stiff peaks. Put the egg yolks, sugar, cornstarch, arrowroot, cream of tartar, baking soda, corn syrup, and vanilla in a separate bowl. Beat well. Fold yolk mixture into the egg whites. Spoon into the cups and bake for 20–25 minutes until firm to the touch. Transfer to a wire rack to cool completely.

Meanwhile, make the filling. Put the egg yolks, sugar, and flour in a bowl and whisk together until creamy. Heat the soy milk in a saucepan until almost boiling. Add the vanilla, then whisk into the egg mixture. Return to the pan and heat gently, stirring, until thick. Pour into a bowl, press plastic wrap over the surface, cool, then chill until firm.

To serve, carefully spoon the soy custard over the cupcakes. Decorate with a strawberry and dust with confectioners' sugar.

Store in an airtight container for up to 3 days, or freeze for up to 3 months.

Makes 1 dozen

Vegan Chocolate Fudge Cupcakes

Just because you're avoiding eggs and dairy, it doesn't mean you need to miss out. This incredibly quick and simple cupcake has a dark, moist texture and a rich, fudgy frosting.

For the cupcakes
1 cup all-purpose flour
¾ tsp. baking soda
4 tbsp. unsweetened cocoa powder
⅔ cup granulated sugar
⅔ cup water
4 tbsp. vegetable oil
1 tbsp. white wine vinegar

For the frosting
2 tbsp. vegetable oil
2 tbsp. unsweetened cocoa powder
2 tbsp. boiling water
1 cup confectioners' sugar, sifted

TIP

Top the frosting with fresh raspberries for a fruity flavor contrast.

Preheat the oven to 350°F (175°C). Place 12 paper baking cups in a muffin pan.

Sift the flour, baking soda, and cocoa into a bowl, then stir in the sugar and make a well in the middle. Pour the oil, vinegar, and water into the well and stir together quickly. Immediately pour the batter into the prepared cups and bake for 20–25 minutes until risen and a skewer inserted in the center comes out clean. Remove pan from the oven and cool for 5 minutes. Then remove the cupcakes and cool on a rack.

To make the frosting, put the oil, cocoa, and boiling water in a heatproof bowl set over a pan of simmering water. Stir to combine, then gradually stir in the sugar and mix for about 2 minutes until thick and glossy. Add a drop or more water if too thick. Pour the frosting over the cupcakes and let it set for a few minutes before serving.

Store in an airtight container for up to 3 days, or freeze for up to 3 months.

Makes 1 dozen

Low-fat Lemon Berry Cupcakes

Simple and summery, these fresh and fruity cupcakes are just the thing if you're watching your weight. These cupcakes are best eaten on the day they're made.

TIP

Make your own lemon curd using the recipe on page 241.

For the cupcakes
3 extra-large eggs
⅓ cup superfine sugar
⅓ cup all-purpose flour, sifted
1 tsp. baking powder
finely grated zest of 1 lemon
3 tbsp. melted butter

To decorate
½ cup (4 oz) fat-free fromage frais
 or fromage blanc
2–3 tbsp. prepared lemon curd
about 1 cup fresh berries, such as
 blueberries, strawberries,
 raspberries, and red currants

Preheat the oven to 350°F (175°C). Place 12 paper baking cups in a muffin pan.

Put the eggs and sugar in a bowl over a pan of barely simmering water, making sure the bowl does not touch the water. Whisk for about 10 minutes until the mixture is thick and pale and leaves a trail when the whisk is lifted out of the bowl.

Sift about three-quarters of the flour over the mixture and fold in. Sift in the remaining flour, sprinkle in the lemon zest, and gradually drizzle in the butter as you fold together.

Spoon the batter into the cups and bake for 20–25 minutes until risen and golden and a skewer inserted in the center comes out clean. Turn out onto a wire rack to cool completely.

Just before serving, stir together the fromage frais and lemon curd, checking the flavor and adding a little more lemon curd if needed. Carefully spread over the cupcakes and decorate with fresh berries.

Store in an airtight container for up to 3 days, or freeze for up to 3 months.

Makes 1 dozen

Gluten-free Yogurt Cupcakes

These light and fluffy gluten-free cupcakes are similar to a cheesecake in taste and texture. Inspired by a classic Moroccan sweet, they are delicious served for dessert.

¼ cup sour cream
1 cup (9 oz) Greek yogurt
1½ tbsp. gluten-free cornstarch,
    dissolved in 1 ½ tbsp. cold water
finely grated zest and juice of
    1 lemon

finely grated zest of 1 orange
3 extra-large eggs, separated
⅓ cup superfine sugar
¼ cup toasted almonds, chopped,
    to decorate

TIP

Serve drizzled with clear honey.

Preheat the oven to 350°F (175°C). Place 12 paper baking cups in a muffin pan.

Stir together the sour cream, yogurt, and cornstarch mixture until well mixed. Fold in the lemon zest and juice and the orange zest. In a separate bowl, whisk together the egg yolks and ¼ cup of the sugar until thick and pale, then stir into the yogurt mixture. In another bowl, whisk the egg whites until they form peaks, then whisk in the remaining sugar. Fold the whites into the yogurt mixture, and spoon into the cups.

Place the muffin pan in a roasting pan. Pour in cold water to reach about halfway up the sides of the muffin pan, then bake for 30–40 minutes. Remove the dish from the oven, sprinkle with the toasted almonds, and let cool. Serve at room temperature or chilled.

Store in an airtight container for up to 3 days, or freeze for up to 3 months.

Makes 1 dozen

Dairy-free Berry Cupcakes

These little treats are wonderful for the lactose-intolerant cupcake lover.
Top each cupcake with a teaspoon of berry jelly.

For the cupcakes
2½ cups mixed fresh berries
   (blueberries, strawberries,
   cranberries, blackberries)
2 cups all-purpose flour
½ cup packed brown sugar

1 tbsp. baking powder
4 tbsp. vegetable oil
2 lightly beaten extra-large eggs

For the topping
½ cup mixed berry jelly

TIP
You could try replacing the same amount of berries for canned peaches.

Preheat the oven to 350˚F (175˚C). Place 12 paper
baking cups in a muffin pan.

In a food processor, purée 1½ cups of the berries until
smooth. In a small bowl, lightly crush the reserved
berries with a fork. In a medium bowl, mix the flour,
sugar, and baking powder.

In a large bowl, beat the oil and eggs. Add the puréed berries
and mix well. Stir in the flour mixture until combined. Fold in the
crushed berries. Spoon the batter into the cups. Bake for
20 minutes. Remove pan from the oven and cool for
5 minutes. Then remove the cupcakes and cool
on a rack.

Store in an airtight container for up to 3 days,
or freeze for up to 3 months.

Makes 1 dozen

Gluten-free Nut & Raisin Cupcakes

Serve these to friends or kids as a treat and they will never know how healthy they are!

1 cup soy bran
1 cup (5 oz) finely ground, roasted macadamia nuts
¾ cup packed brown sugar
1 tbsp. baking powder
2 lightly beaten large eggs
4 tbsp. vegetable oil

4 tbsp. sweet butter, melted and cooled
¾ cup milk
½ cup (3½ oz) raisins
4 tbsp. roughly chopped macadamia nuts

TIP

Cherries also work well as a replacement for the raisins.

Preheat the oven to 375°F (190°C). Grease a 12-cup muffin pan.

In a medium bowl, mix the bran, nuts, sugar, and baking powder. In a large bowl, beat the eggs, oil, butter, and milk. Add the flour, mixing until nearly combined. Fold in the raisins and macadamia nuts.

Spoon the mixture into the prepared pan. Bake for about 20 minutes. Remove pan from the oven and cool for 5 minutes. Then remove the cupcakes and cool on a rack.

Store in an airtight container for up to 3 days, or freeze for up to 3 months.

Makes 1 dozen

Avocado & Olive Oil Cupcakes

Avocados contain a host of essential oils, vitamins, and minerals—all beneficial for the body's nervous system.

2 medium hass avocados, peeled
   and roughly chopped
1 tsp. lemon juice
2½ cups all-purpose flour
pinch of salt
1 tbsp. baking powder

2 lightly beaten extra-large eggs
1 cup milk
4 tbsp. extra virgin olive oil
4 tbsp. sweet butter, melted
1½ tbsp. lemon zest
1 tsp. freshly ground black pepper

TIP

For a juicy addition, try adding 3 tablespoons chopped sun-dried tomatoes to the batter after the flour has been added.

Preheat the oven to 400°F (200°C). Grease a 12-cup muffin pan.

Place the avocados in a bowl with the lemon juice. Crush lightly with a fork. In a medium bowl, mix the flour, salt, and baking powder. Beat the remaining ingredients in a large bowl. Add the flour mixture, stirring until nearly combined. Fold in the avocados. Do not over-mix.

Spoon the mixture into the prepared pan. Bake for 20 minutes. Remove pan from the oven and cool for 5 minutes. Then remove the cupcakes and cool on a rack. Store in an airtight container for up to 2 days or freeze for up to 3 months.

Makes 1 dozen

Chocolate Meringue Cupcakes

Meringue is the ideal dessert for anyone on a gluten-free diet, and these simple cupcakes topped with strawberries and cream make the perfect choice.

For the meringues
1 cup toasted hazelnuts
1½ cups superfine sugar
5 large egg whites
2 tbsp. Dutch-process cocoa, sieved
2 tsp. white wine vinegar

For the filling
½ cup whipping cream
1 cup fresh strawberries, hulled and sliced

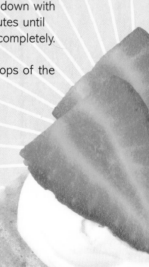

TIP
You could also try raspberry, blueberry, or grape toppings.

Preheat the oven to 375°F (190°C). Place 24 paper baking cups in a muffin pan.

Put the nuts in a food processor and process until finely ground. Add about one-quarter of the sugar and stir together, then set aside. Whisk the egg whites until they form peaks, then gradually whisk in the remaining sugar until glossy and stiff. Gently fold in the nuts, cocoa, and vinegar.

Spoon or pipe the mixture into the cups and press the centers down with the back of a spoon to make a dip. Bake for about 20–25 minutes until firm. Turn off the oven and leave the meringues inside to cool completely.

To serve, whip the cream to stiff peaks and spread it over the tops of the meringues. Top each with a sliced strawberry.

Store in an airtight container for up to 2 days, or freeze for up to 3 months.

Makes 2 dozen

Fly-away Chocolate Orange Cupcakes

This recipe has only a small amount of flour to give the cupcakes a
light, fluffy texture.

½ cup Dutch-process cocoa powder
¾ cup packed light brown sugar
3 tbsp. all-purpose flour
4½ tsp. baking powder
pinch of salt
2 tsp. orange extract
¾ cup fat-free milk

1 cup chopped bittersweet
  chocolate
1 lightly beaten egg
3 egg whites
¼ tsp. cream of tartar
⅓ cup superfine sugar
cocoa powder and confectioners'
  sugar, for dusting

TIP

Try adding 2 teaspoons
cinnamon to the
dry ingredients.

Preheat the oven to 350°F (175°C). Place 12 paper baking cups
in a muffin pan.

In a heavy saucepan, combine the cocoa, sugar, flour, baking powder, salt,
orange extract, and milk over a gentle heat. Stir until the sugar dissolves, being
careful not to burn the mixture. Remove from the heat, and gradually
stir in the chocolate until it melts. Whisk in the egg. Transfer to a
large bowl to cool, and set aside.

In a medium bowl, combine the egg whites and cream
of tartar. Beat with an electric mixer until soft peaks
form. Gradually add the sugar, one-third at a time,
beating for 1 minute after each addition. Using a metal
spoon, fold the egg whites into the chocolate, making
sure not to over-mix. Spoon the mixture into the cups.
Bake for 20 minutes.

Remove the pan from the oven and cool for 5 minutes.
Then remove the cupcakes, dust with cocoa powder and
confectioners' sugar, and serve immediately.

Store in an airtight container for up to 2 days, or freeze for
up to 3 months.

Makes 1 dozen

Apple Bran Cupcakes

These cupcakes are great for children because they contain a host of essential nutrients and vitamins—and yet they taste delicious.

4 cups oat bran
1 cup all-purpose flour
1½ tsp. baking powder
½ cup packed brown sugar
pinch of salt
2 tsp. cinnamon
2 cups milk

4 tbsp. vegetable oil
2 lightly beaten extra-large eggs
2 tbsp. honey
2 cups shredded carrot
1 cup shredded apple
1½ cups (9 oz) raisins

TIP

You could make these into vegetable cupcakes by replacing 2 cups apple with 2 cups cooked mixed zucchini and carrots.

Preheat the oven to 350°F (175°C). Grease a 12-cup muffin pan.

In a large bowl, combine the dry ingredients with a spoon. In a separate bowl, beat the milk, oil, eggs, and honey with an electric mixer until combined. Stir in the shredded carrot, apple, and raisins. Add the dry ingredients and stir until just combined. Spoon the mixture into the prepared pan.

Bake in the oven for 20 minutes. Remove pan from the oven and cool for 5 minutes. Then remove the muffins and cool on a rack.

Store in an airtight container for up to 3 days, or freeze for up to 3 months.

Makes 1 dozen

Triple Chocolate & Orange Cupcakes

You would never know that these are low-fat—who said dieting had to be boring?

For the cupcakes
2⅔ cups all-purpose flour
1 cup superfine sugar
1 tbsp. baking powder
2 tbsp. Dutch-process cocoa powder
2 lightly beaten extra-large eggs
½ cup sunflower oil
¾ cup fat-free milk
1 tsp. vanilla extract

For the frosting
2 tbsp. butter, softened
1½ cups confectioner's sugar, sifted
⅓ cup Dutch-process cocoa powder
½ tsp. orange extract
½ tsp. vanilla extract
4 tbsp. fat-free millk
silver sprinkles, to decorate

TIP

Serve with strawberries to get the wonderful contrast of fruit and chocolate.

Preheat the oven to 350°F (175°C). Place 12 paper baking cups in a muffin pan.

In a medium bowl, mix the flour, sugar, and baking powder with a spoon. In a large bowl, combine the eggs, oil, milk, and vanilla with an electric mixer and beat until combined. Add the flour mixture and stir until just combined. Do not over-mix. Divide the mixture into two and add the cocoa powder to one half. Spoon the batter without cocoa into the cups. Add a layer of the chocolate batter on top. Bake for 20 minutes. Remove pan from the oven and cool for 5 minutes. Then remove the muffins and cool on a rack.

For the frosting, combine all the ingredients except the milk. Add the milk slowly, beating with an electric mixer to make a firm but spreadable mixture. Spoon the frosting onto the cooled muffins, and decorate with silver sprinkles.

Store unfrosted in an airtight container for up to 3 days, or freeze for up to 3 months.

Makes 1 dozen

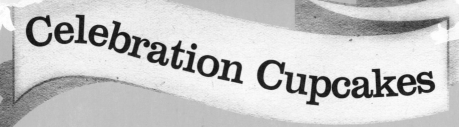

Celebration Cupcakes

If you have an occasion to celebrate, there
is a cupcake to accompany it. Among others,
the perfect Halloween, St. Patrick's Day,
Thanksgiving, Valentine's Day, Mother's Day,
and Easter recipes are featured. Find
a special cupcake for all seasons!

Celebration Cupcakes

Celebration cupcakes are the most fun to make and eat. The colorful frostings and decorations appeal to children, but adults love these cupcakes too! It's not all about appearance; these recipes are utterly delicious with some reserved for adult-only celebrations. If you like the mouthwatering flavors of a particular recipe, it's easy to adapt these cupcakes for a variety of special days.

Halloween cupcakes are simple, sugary, and totally satisfying. If these go down well, make a white frosting then decorate with red and blue sprinkles for the 4th of July. Similarly, Easter cupcakes become thanksgiving treats by topping with candy corn. If you love winter-themed recipes but aren't sure about coconut, decorate Berry Snowflake Cupcakes with mini marshmallows; mix and match pink and white for the desired effect.

Fruit cakes are traditional at Christmas, whether it's the rich and thick varieties or light and fluffy Italian panettone. Dried mixed fruit zest isn't for everyone, but these recipes feel just as traditional using dried cranberries instead. The different textures ensure a range of perfect holiday delights for you to choose from. No matter the occasion, you'll love making celebration cupcakes.

Halloween Cupcakes

These fun cupcakes will brighten up any kid's party.

For the cupcakes
3 extra-large eggs
¾ cup superfine sugar
1½ cups all-purpose
  flour
2 tsp. baking powder
¾ cup sweet butter
  or margarine

For the frosting
1 cup (2 sticks) sweet
  butter, softened
1 cup confectioners'
  sugar, sifted
3 tbsp. Dutch-process
  cocoa powder or a
  few drops orange

food coloring
1 tbsp. milk
orange and yellow
  sprinkles

TIP

Decorate them with fun icing to your heart's desire—make them as gruesome as you can!

Preheat the oven to 350°F (175°C).
Line two 12-cup muffin pans with paper
baking cups.

Put the cupcake ingredients in a large
bowl and beat with an electric mixer for
3 to 4 minutes, until the mixture is smooth
and pale. Divide the mixture between the
cups. Bake for 15 minutes until well risen
and golden brown. Remove from the oven and
cool for 5 minutes. Transfer to a wire rack
to cool completely.

Combine the butter, confectioners' sugar, cocoa
powder or orange food coloring, and milk in a large
bowl and beat until smooth. Spoon into a frosting bag
fitted with a medium star nozzle and pipe a large swirl of
frosting on top of each cupcake.

Decorate the cupcakes with orange and yellow sprinkles.
Store in an airtight container for up to 2 days.

Makes 2 dozen

Amaretto Wedding Cupcakes

These cupcakes are perfect for a home-style wedding. Each of your guests can take one home as a memento of the day.

For the cupcakes
1 cup (2 sticks) sweet butter, softened
1 cup superfine sugar
2 cups all-purpose flour
3 tsp. baking powder
4 large eggs

1 tsp. vanilla extract
3 tbsp. Amaretto

For the frosting
½ cup confectioners' sugar
2 tbsp. lemon juice
18 frosted roses

TIP

See page 29 to make your own frosted roses.

Preheat the oven to 350˚F (175˚C). Place 18 paper baking cups in muffin pans.

Combine all the cupcake ingredients in a large bowl and beat with an electric mixer until smooth and pale, about 2–3 minutes.

Spoon the batter into the cups. Bake for 20 minutes. Remove pans from the oven and cool for 5 minutes. Then remove the cupcakes and cool on a rack. Once cooled, drizzle the Amaretto over the cupcakes before icing them.

To make the frosting, sift the confectioners' sugar into a medium bowl. Add the lemon juice gradually, until it holds its shape. Spread onto the cupcakes, and top with roses.

Store unfrosted in an airtight container for up to 3 days, or freeze for up to 3 months.

Makes 1½ dozen

Christmas Fruit Cupcakes

These are deliciously mini takes on a moist fruitcake.

1⅔ cups all-purpose flour, plus
 a little extra for dusting
2 tsp. baking powder
1 tsp. ground cinnamon
1 tsp. apple pie spice
1 tsp. ground ginger
pinch of salt
½ cup (1 stick) sweet butter, plus
 a little extra for greasing
½ cup soft light brown sugar,
 lightly packed
1 can crushed pineapple
1 cup raisins, lightly packed

1 cup golden raisins, lightly packed
1 cup candied ginger, finely
 chopped
½ cup candied cherries, chopped
½ cup orange and lemon peel
2 extra-large eggs, lightly beaten
pecan halves and candied cherries
 for decoration
2–3 tbsp. honey, apricot jelly or
 marmalade for glazing

TIP

Surround a chocolate log with these cupcakes for a twist on the traditional festive dessert.

Preheat the oven to 325°F (160°C). Line two 12-cup muffin pans with paper baking cups.

Sift the flour, baking soda, ground cinnamon, mixed spice, ground ginger, and salt into a bowl and set aside. Melt the butter and sugar in a saucepan until the sugar has dissolved, stirring frequently. Add the pineapple with its juices and stir in dried fruits and ginger. Bring to a boil and simmer for 3 minutes, stirring. Remove from the heat and cool.

When cool, add the fruit mixture to the flour mixture with the candied cherries and mixed orange and lemon peel. Stir in the beaten eggs and spoon into the cups and smooth the tops. Arrange 3 pecans and a cherry half on the top of each cupcake, pressing gently into the batter. Bake for 30–45 minutes. If the cakes color too quickly, lower the temperature slightly and cover the top of the pan with a piece of foil. Remove to a wire rack to cool for 30 minutes before unmolding and cooling completely. Melt the honey or marmalade in a pan and brush over the tops.

Makes 2 dozen

Panettone Cupcake Puddings

Try this rich and robust cupcake recipe for an unusual twist on the classic bread pudding.

5 cups strong white
   bread flour
½ tsp. salt
1 tsp. dried yeast
4 fl. oz) lukewarm milk
2 large eggs
2 large egg yolks

5 ½ oz sweet butter softened
2 ½ oz superfine sugar
4 oz chopped mixed peel
2½ oz raisins
butter for the cases and
   for brushing
confectioners' sugar for dusting

TIP

The best way to knead is to press and stretch the dough away from you, give it a quarter turn and repeat.

Preheat the oven to 350°F (180°C). Sift the flour into a mixing bowl, add the salt and make a well in the center. In another bowl, whisk together the yeast, milk, and whole eggs. Pour into the well, fold in a little of the surrounding flour to make a batter that sits in the well. Leave to rest for 30 minutes. Add the egg yolks, butter, and sugar and mix them and the rest of the flour into the batter with a fork. Then bind everything together into a ball with your hands.

Knead the dough for 5 minutes. Leave to rest in a warm place for 1½–2 hours or until doubled in size. Scatter over the peel and raisins and gently knead these in.

Butter the panettone cases. Divide the dough into 12 and place in the cases—avoid leaving dried fruit exposed on the surface of the breads as this may burn during cooking and turn bitter. Set aside, covered with a dry tea towel, and rest for 1 hour.

Brush the tops of the breads with melted butter and bake for 20 minutes. Dust with confectioners' sugar, if you like, before serving. Store in an airtight container for up to 3 days.

Makes 1 dozen

Carnival Cupcakes

Our version of the classic Mardi Gras "king cake." The colors traditionally used on the cake represent justice, faith, and power.

For the cupcakes
1 cup (2 sticks) sweet butter, softened
1 cup superfine sugar
2 cups all-purpose flour
3 tsp. baking powder
4 large eggs
1 tsp. vanilla extract

For the frosting
2½ cups confectioners' sugar
2 tbsp. lemon juice
2 tbsp. gold-colored sugar
2 tbsp. green-colored sugar
2 tbsp. purple-colored sugar

TIP

For a white chocolate addition, fold ½ cup white chocolate chips into the creamed batter.

Preheat the oven to 350˚F (175˚C). Place 18 paper baking cups in muffin pans. Combine all the cupcake ingredients in a large bowl and beat with an electric mixer until smooth and pale, about 2–3 minutes.

Spoon the batter into the cups. Bake for 20 minutes. Remove pans from the oven and cool for 5 minutes. Then remove the cupcakes and cool on a rack.

To make the frosting, sift the confectioners' sugar in a medium bowl. Slowly add the lemon juice until the mixture becomes firm but spreadable. Spread onto the cupcakes, and sprinkle with the colored sugar.

Store unfrosted in an airtight container for up to 3 days, or freeze for up to 3 months.

Makes 1½ **dozen**

Easter Cupcakes

If you're not a big fan of hollow chocolate eggs and bunnies, this recipe is for you.

For the cupcakes
4 large eggs
⅔ cup superfine sugar
1 cup all-purpose flour
1½ tsp. baking powder
1 cup dry unsweetened flaked
  coconut
½ cup (1 stick) sweet butter, melted

For the frosting
½ cup sweet butter
1¾ cups sifted confectioners' sugar
2 tbsp. cocoa powder
chocolate eggs to decorate

TIP

Present in a little basket with little toy chicks for a festive gift.

Preheat the oven to 400°F (200°C). Line two 12-cup muffin pans with paper baking cups.

Combine the eggs and sugar in a large bowl and beat with an electric mixer for 2–3 minutes, until smooth. Sift the flour and baking powder over the top of the creamed mixture. Using a metal spoon, lightly fold in the flour using a figure-of-8 movement. Add the coconut and melted butter and continue to fold in gently. Divide the mixture between the cups.

Bake for 10 minutes, or until well risen and golden brown. Remove from the oven and cool for 5 minutes. Transfer to a wire rack to cool completely.

To make the frosting, beat the butter, confectioners' sugar, and cocoa together. Pipe the frosting in a swirl on top of each cake and decorate with chocolate eggs.

Store in an airtight container for up to 4 days.

Makes 2 dozen

Mother's Day Cupcakes

These light, fresh, lemony cupcakes are perfect for celebrating Mother's Day. Alternatively, make them as a gift to take to a spring lunch party or enjoy them with guests.

For the cupcakes
1½ sticks butter, at room
    temperature
¾ cup superfine sugar
finely grated zest of 1 lemon
3 extra-large eggs
scant 1¼ cups all-purpose flour
1½ tsp. baking powder

For the frosting
1½ cups (9½ oz) cream cheese
generous ⅓ cup confectioners'
    sugar, sifted
finely grated zest of 1 lemon, plus
    2 tsp. juice
3 tbsp. prepared lemon curd
edible flower petals, to decorate

TIP

Different edible flowers to try are pansies, marigolds, nasturtiums, and lavender.

Preheat the oven to 350°F (175°C). Line two 12-cup muffin pans with paper baking cups.

Beat together the butter, sugar, and lemon zest until pale and creamy, then beat in the eggs one at a time. Sift the flour and baking powder over the bowl, then fold in. Divide the batter between the cups. Bake for 15–20 minutes until risen and golden. Turn out onto a wire rack and let cool completely.

To make the frosting, beat together the cream cheese, confectioners' sugar, lemon zest, and lemon juice until smooth and creamy. Spread lemon curd over the cupcakes, then carefully spread over the frosting. Decorate with flowers.

Store unfrosted in an airtight container for up to 2 days, or freeze for up to 3 months.

Makes 2 dozen

Christmas Cranberry Cupcakes

These light, fruity cupcakes, which combine the delicate flavor of pear with the sharp tang of cranberries, make a wonderful alternative to a traditional fruit cupcake.

For the cupcake
1½ sticks butter, at room
    temperature
¾ cup superfine sugar
3 extra-large eggs
1⅓ cups all-purpose flour
1½ tsp. baking powder
¾ tsp. apple pie spice

2 pears, peeled, cored, and diced
½ cup dried cranberries

For the frosting
2 cups mascarpone
½ cup confectioners' sugar, sifted
fresh cranberries and small holly
    leaves, to decorate

TIP

For an even more festive taste, add 3 pieces of stem ginger in syrup with the pear and cranberries.

Preheat the oven to 350°F (175°C). Line two 12-cup muffin pans with paper baking cups.

Beat together the butter and sugar until pale and creamy, then beat in the eggs one at a time. Sift the flour, baking powder, and apple pie spice over the bowl, then fold in. Fold in the pears and cranberries.

Divide the mixture between the cups, smoothing the tops with the back of a spoon. Bake for 15–20 minutes until risen and golden. Transfer to a wire rack and let cool completely.

To make the frosting, beat together the mascarpone and confectioners' sugar until smooth and creamy. Spread over the cakes. Decorate with fresh cranberries and holly leaves. Store unfrosted in an airtight container for up to 2 days, or freeze for up to 3 months.

Makes 2 dozen

Christening Cupcakes

These delicate little cupcakes are perfect for the special day of a Christening.

For the cupcakes
2 tbsp. butter
1⅛ cups all-purpose flour
2 tsp. baking powder
1 extra-large egg
⅙ cup superfine sugar
5 tbsp. buttermilk
3 tbsp. sour cream
3 tbsp. caramel sauce
   (store-bought product)

For the icing
2 cups confectioners' sugar
1–3 tbsp. evaporated milk
sugar flowers

TIP

If you are feeling particularly creative, why not make the flowers yourself using fondant sheets.

Preheat the oven to 350°F (175°C). Line a muffin pan with paper cases.

Melt the butter. Mix the flour and baking powder in a bowl. Whisk together the egg, sugar, melted butter, buttermilk, sour cream, and caramel sauce. Quickly mix in the dry ingredients with an electric hand mixer. Divide the mixture between the cups and bake for about 20 minutes. Take out and let rest in the pan for 5–10 minutes, then take out of the pan and cool on a wire rack.

Mix the confectioners' sugar with the evaporated milk to make a thick frosting. Spread on the cupcakes, decorate with sugar flowers, and leave to dry. Store unfrosted in an airtight container for up to 2 days, or freeze for up to 3 months.

Makes 1 dozen

Birthday Gateau Cupcakes

This chocolate gateau is rich and creamy with the refreshing bite of fresh fruit.

For the cupcakes
9 oz bittersweet chocolate
1½ sticks butter, diced
1 cup superfine sugar
3 extra-large eggs
generous ⅔ cup all-purpose flour
2 tbsp. instant coffee dissolved in
   2 tbsp. boiling water

For the frosting
2 cups semisweet chocolate,
   chopped
⅓ cup (⅔ stick) sweet butter
colored sprinkles and silver
   sprinkles, to decorate

TIP
You could try topping with slices of kiwi fruit.

Preheat the oven to 325°F (160°C). Line a 12-cup muffin pan with paper baking cups.

Break the chocolate into pieces and put in a heatproof bowl with the butter. Place the bowl over a pan of gently simmering water and heat gently until the chocolate and butter have melted. Remove from the heat and let cool. Stir in the sugar, then beat in the eggs, one at a time. Sift the flour over the mixture, then fold in. Stir in the coffee. Tip the mixture into the cups and bake for 20–30 minutes until firm on top, with a very slight wobble in the center. Let cool in the pan.

For the frosting, melt the chocolate with the butter in a double boiler or over a simmering pan of water, stirring to combine. Remove from the heat once melted and thickened, and let cool. Spread the chocolate frosting over the cakes. Decorate with silver candies and sprinkles.

Makes 1 dozen

Berry Snowflake Cupcakes

These cupcakes are delightful for a Christmas gathering. You can serve them on Christmas Eve when Santa's sleigh has set off and the kids are tucked into bed.

TIP

If you remove the sherry, the cupcakes will look less pink and will resemble a snowball.

For the cupcakes
1 cup (2 sticks) sweet butter, softened
1 cup superfine sugar
2 cups all-purpose flour
3 tsp. baking powder
4 large eggs
1 tsp. vanilla extract
4 tbsp. dried mixed fruit, such as cranberries or cherries

For the frosting
½ cup (1 stick) sweet butter, softened
2 cups confectioners' sugar, sifted
1 tsp. vanilla extract
2 tsp. pale dry sherry
4 tbsp. sweetened coconut

Preheat the oven to 350°F (175°C). Place 18 paper baking cups in muffin pans.

Combine all the cupcake ingredients in a large bowl, except the dried berries, and beat with an electric mixer until smooth and pale, about 2–3 minutes. Stir in the dried berries. Spoon the batter into the cups. Bake for 20 minutes. Remove pans from the oven and cool for 5 minutes. Then remove the cupcakes and cool on a rack.

For the coconut frosting, beat the butter, confectioners' sugar, vanilla, and sherry in a medium bowl until smooth and creamy. Spread on top of the cupcakes. Sprinkle a little coconut on top to resemble snowflakes.

Store unfrosted in an airtight container for up to 3 days, or freeze for up to 3 months.

Makes 1½ dozen

Strawberries & Ice Cream Cupcakes

Perfect to celebrate the beginning of summer.

For the cupcakes
1 cup (2 sticks) sweet butter,
  softened
1 cup superfine sugar
2 cups self-rising flour
1½ tsp. baking powder

4 large eggs
1 tsp. vanilla extract

For the decoration
2 cups vanilla ice cream
9 strawberries, halved

TIP

You could place the cut out pieces of cake at an angle on top of the icecream for an artistic touch.

Preheat the oven to 350°F (175°C). Place 18 paper baking cups in muffin pans.

Place all the ingredients for the cupcakes in a medium bowl and beat with an electric mixer until smooth and pale, about 2 to 3 minutes. Spoon the mixture into the cups. Bake for 20 minutes.

Remove the pans from the oven and cool for 5 minutes, then remove the cupcakes and cool on a rack. Cut a small circle on the top of each cake. Using a teaspoon, carefully scoop the cake out from beneath it. Using a melon baller, press a tiny scoop of ice cream into the hole of each cupcake. Top each with a half strawberry.

Serve immediately or store undecorated in an airtight container for up to 3 days, or freeze for up to 3 months.

Makes 1½ dozen

Christmas Holly Cupcakes

Nothing is more iconic of Christmas than a holly leaf, and these cute cupcakes will be a great gift for an avid bake-enthusiast.

For the cupcakes
1 cup (2 sticks) sweet butter, softened
1 cup superfine sugar
2 cups all-purpose flour
3 tsp. baking powder
4 large eggs
1 tsp. vanilla extract

For the frosting
½ cup (1 stick) sweet butter
2 cups confectioners' sugar, sifted
1 tbsp. lemon juice
2 oz ready-to-roll fondant sheet
a little confectioners' sugar for dusting
a few drops green and red food coloring

Preheat the oven to 350˚F (175˚C). Place 18 paper baking cups in muffin pans.

Place all the ingredients for the cupcakes in a medium bowl and beat with an electric mixer until smooth and pale, about 2–3 minutes. Spoon the mixture into the cups. Bake for 20 minutes. Remove the pans from the oven and cool for 5 minutes, then remove the cupcakes and cool on a rack.

Beat the frosting ingredients together in a bowl until smooth and creamy. Spoon over the cupcakes.

For the decoration, cut the fondant into two pieces. On a lightly dusted surface, kneed the green food coloring into one piece until evenly distributed. Roll out thinly, then cut out small leaf shapes with a cutter. Kneed the red food coloring into the other piece of fondant, then pull off small pieces and roll into berry-sized balls. Decorate the cupcakes with the fondant leaves and berries.

Makes 1½ dozen

Garden Party Cupcakes

The sun is shining, and everything you eat needs to be colorful and happy to match your mood—these jolly little cakes will make everyone smile!

TIP

Daisies are not edible, so use them to decorate. For some edible flowers you could also try, see page 29.

For the cupcakes
1 cup (2 sticks) sweet butter, softened
1 cup superfine sugar
2 cups all-purpose flour
3 tsp. baking powder
4 large eggs
1 tsp. vanilla extract

For the frosting
½ cup (1 stick) sweet butter
2 cups confectioners' sugar, sifted
1 tsp. vanilla extract
3 tbsp. yellow sprinkles and ½ cup daisies, rinsed, to decorate

Preheat the oven to 350°F (175°C). Place 18 paper baking cups in muffin pans.

Place all the ingredients for the cupcakes in a medium bowl and beat with an electric mixer until smooth and pale, about 2–3 minutes. Spoon the mixture into the cups. Bake for 20 minutes. Remove the pans from the oven and cool for 5 minutes, then remove the cupcakes and cool on a rack. For the frosting, beat the ingredients together then spread over the cupcakes.

To decorate, sprinkle the yellow candies on the top of each cupcake. Cut a daisy leaving a 1-in. stem, and push into the frosting carefully.

Serve immediately or store unfrosted in an airtight container for up to 3 days, or freeze for up to 3 months.

Makes 1½ **dozen**

Raspberry Ripple Cupcakes

For a birthday cupcake batch, you want to go all out. Try these extra-special colorful cakes.

For the cupcakes
¾ cup (1½ sticks) butter, at room temperature
¾ cup superfine sugar
3 extra-large eggs
1¼ cups all-purpose flour
1½ tsp. baking powder
1 tsp. vanilla extract
3 tbsp. frozen raspberries, thawed

For the frosting
1 cup cream cheese, softened
1½ cups confectioners' sugar, sifted
1 tbsp. lemon juice
1 tsp. vanilla extract
20 fresh raspberries, to decorate

TIP
Try with different ripples—strawberry and apricot works really well too.

Preheat the oven to 350°F (175°C). Line two 12-cup muffin pans with paper baking cups.

Heat the raspberries gently in a pan over a low heat, stirring, until hot and starting to break up. Leave to cool completely.

Beat together the butter and sugar until pale and creamy, then beat in the eggs one at a time. Sift the flour over the top, then fold in. Stir in the vanilla extract, then sprinkle over the cooled raspberries. Using a palate knife, gently swirl the cooled raspberries into the batter, taking care not to mix them in fully.

Divide the batter between the cups. Bake for 15–20 minutes until well risen and golden brown. Remove from the oven and cool for 5 minutes. Transfer to a wire rack to cool completely.

For the frosting, beat the ingredients together, spoon over the cooled cupcakes, then decorate each with a raspberry. Serve immediately or store unfrosted in an airtight container for up to 3 days, or freeze for up to 3 months.

Makes 2 dozen

Adult Cupcakes

A collection of cupcakes for adults—some sinfully calorific, others just a little bit tipsy.

Adult Cupcakes

Adult cupcakes are the richest, the naughtiest, and the most devilishly delicious recipes that are best kept secret from little cherubs. Alcoholic ingredients give these treats an entirely new dimension of flavor, and this chapter holds the ultimate indulgences for late-night cravings. Some require a sophisticated palette, and others need a fire-proof tongue. Whatever your preference, there are variations to tone them down or to turn up the heat.

If you love the flavor but not the buzz, rum raisin works well with rum flavoring from the baking aisle, but for a more authentic taste, soak the raisins in rum for a day before making the cupcakes. Millionaire's Cupcakes will satisfy a lifetime of sugar cravings, so sensitive teeth sufferers might want to skip the caramel; if you're undeterred by sugary goodness, serve in cupcake cases made from real chocolate. These are available from all good baking stores.

For those who love subtle flavors, the Fennel Cupcakes, batter made with couscous, and spiced recipes with aromatic herbs are both delicious and refreshingly chic. This chapter proves that cupcakes can tickle any adult fancy.

Walnut–banana Chocolate Cupcakes

A timeless combination for a very grown-up kind of tea party.

¼ cup sweet butter
¾ cup superfine sugar
1 extra-large egg
2 bananas, mashed

2½ cups all-purpose flour
3 tsp. baking powder
1¾ cup chopped walnuts
½ cup semisweet chocolate chips
½ cup milk

TIP

You could replace the walnuts for the same amount of chopped cashew nuts or Brazil nuts.

Preheat the oven to 325°F (160°C). Place 15 paper baking cups in muffin pans.

Beat the butter and sugar in a medium bowl until smooth. Beat in the egg and the banana.

In a separate bowl, combine the flour, baking powder, walnuts, and chocolate chips and stir well. Beat the nutty mixture into the creamed mixture, and stir in the buttermilk. Divde the batter between the cups and bake for 20 minutes until well risen and a wooden pick inserted into the center comes out clean. Remove from the oven and transfer to a wire rack to cool.

Store in an airtight container for up to 4 days.

Makes 1 dozen

Rum & Raisin Cupcakes

Use dark rum in this recipe to give these cupcakes a warm Caribbean feel. Enjoy warm for dessert. These go well with a side of custard or rum-flavored cream.

For the cupcakes
½ cup (3½ oz) raisins
3 tbsp. dark rum
1 cup (2 sticks) sweet butter, softened
1 cup superfine sugar
2 cups all-purpose flour
2½ tsp. baking powder
4 large eggs

For the glaze
⅔ cups melted sweet butter
2 tbsp. vanilla
4 cups confectioners' sugar
4 tbsp. light rum

TIP

You can make these work in cupcake cases too—divide the mix into 18 paper cases and bake for 20–25 minutes.

Soak the raisins in the rum for 2–3 hours or overnight to soften them. Drain.

Preheat the oven to 350°F (175°C). Lightly grease ten 6-oz ramekins. Combine all the cupcake ingredients in a large bowl and beat with an electric mixer until smooth and pale, about 2–3 minutes. Stir in the soaked raisins. Spoon the batter into the ramekins. Bake for 30 minutes, or until a toothpick inserted into the center of a cupcake comes out clean. Then remove the cupcakes and cool on a rack.

To make the glaze, mix together the melted butter, vanilla, and sugar. Stir in the rum, a tablespoon at a time, until the glaze is spreading consistency. Spoon over cupcakes.

Store unfrosted in an airtight container for up to 3 days, or freeze for up to 3 months.

Makes 1½ dozen

Guinness Cupcakes

Guinness is the perfect beer for desserts because of its distinct chocolate and coffee notes. Pairing it with chocolate is the obvious choice, but this fruit combination is an unusual taste sensation where you can really taste the Guinness.

⅔ cup raisins, soaked overnight in Guinness
½ cup candied peel, soaked
1⅓ cups golden raisins, soaked
1 stick (4 oz) sweet butter
1 cup brown sugar
3 extra-large eggs, beaten

1¼ cups all-purpose flour
2½ tsp. baking powder
pinch of salt
½ tsp. apple pie spice
¼ cup candied cherries
⅔ cup Guinness or dark beer, plus extra for soaking

> **TIP**
>
> Add a Classic Buttercream frosting from page 232 for a white head that Guinness is famous for.

Soak the raisins and the peel in the Guinness overnight. Preheat the oven to 350°F (175°C). Place 18 paper baking cups in muffin pans.

Beat the butter and sugar until the sugar is dissolved. Beat in the eggs. Add the flour, baking powder, salt, apple pie spice, cherries, and the soaked dried fruit. Finally mix in the Guinness. Pour the batter into the prepared cups. Bake for 1 hour until firm in the center.

Store unfrosted in an airtight container for up to 3 days, or freeze for up to 3 months.

Makes 1½ **dozen**

Kicked-up Chili Pineapple Cupcakes

These cupcakes melt in the mouth and are the perfect teatime treat.

For the cupcakes
1 cup (2 sticks) sweet butter,
  softened
1 cup superfine sugar
2 cups all-purpose flour
2 tsp. baking powder
4 large eggs
1 tsp. vanilla extract
1 cup drained crushed pineapple
1 tsp. seeded and finely chopped
  chili pepper

For the frosting
1 cup cream cheese, softened
1½ cups confectioners' sugar, sifted
1 tbsp. lemon juice
1 tsp. vanilla extract
½ cup (3½ oz) chopped walnuts

TIP
Add ½ cup sweetened shredded coconut to the mixture after it has been creamed.

Preheat the oven to 350°F (175°C). Place 18 paper baking cups in muffin pans.

Combine all the cupcake ingredients, except the pineapple and chili, in a large bowl and beat with an electric mixer for about 2–3 minutes. Stir in the pineapple and chili. Spoon the batter into the cups. Bake for 20 minutes. Remove pans from the oven and cool for 5 minutes. Then remove the cupcakes and cool on a rack.

To make the frosting, slowly beat the cream cheese and confectioners' sugar in a large bowl with an electric mixer until creamy and soft. Add the lemon juice and vanilla, and beat briskly until well combined. Spread the frosting onto the cooled cupcakes and garnish with the chopped walnuts.

Store unfrosted in an airtight container for 2–3 days, or freeze for up to 3 months.

Makes 1½ dozen

Passion Fruit & Chocolate Cupcakes

This zingy combination of flavors really is hard to beat. Using fresh-squeezed orange juice in the frosting will give it a delicate orange color and the passion fruit will add an extra flavor.

TIP

If you prefer, you could replace the grated chocolate with the same amount of passion fruit seeds.

For the cupcakes
11-oz can mandarin segments, drained
2 cups all-purpose flour
2 tsp. baking powder
½ tsp. ground cinnamon
1 tbsp. finely grated orange zest
½ cup superfine sugar
¼ cup (½ stick) sweet butter, melted

1 extra-large egg
5 tbsp. milk
½ cup semisweet chocolate chips

For the frosting
2 tbsp. orange juice
½ cup confectioners' sugar
1 tbsp. passion fruit seeds
1 tbsp. grated chocolate

Preheat the oven to 350°F (175°C). Line a muffin pan with 10 paper baking cups.

Roughly chop the mandarin segments and set aside. Combine the flour, baking powder, cinnamon, orange zest, and sugar in a medium bowl and stir well. In a separate bowl beat the butter, egg, and milk. Stir into the flour mixture until just combined.

Stir in the chopped mandarin segments and chocolate chips and divide the batter between the muffin cups. Bake for 20–25 minutes until well risen and a wooden pick inserted into the center comes out clean. Remove from the oven and cool for 10 minutes.

To make the frosting, combine the orange juice with enough confectioners' sugar to form a smooth paste. Stir in the seeds and grated chocolate. Drizzle the frosting over the cupcakes. Transfer to a wire rack to set. Store in an airtight container for up to 4 days. Freezing is not recommended.

Makes 10 cupcakes

Boozy Berry Cupcakes

These fruity cupcakes turn a lovely pink color and are lower in fat, because they use oil rather than butter.

For the cupcake
3 extra-large eggs
8 fl. oz vegetable oil
1½ cups superfine sugar
2 cups frozen mixed red berries
3 tbsp. fruit liqueur, such as
   blackcurrant, blackberry, or
   strawberry
4 oz white chocolate chips

1 lb. all-purpose flour
2 tsp. baking powder

For the frosting
1 cup cream cheese, softened
1½ cups confectioners' sugar,
   sifted
1 tsp. red food coloring
2 tbsp. white sprinkles

TIP

Try decorating with melted white chocolate, allowing it to set on top.

Preheat the oven to 350°F (175°C). Line a muffin pan with 24 paper baking cups.

Combine the eggs, oil, sugar, half the fruit and liqueur, and the chocolate in a bowl and beat well. Gradually add the flour and baking powder to the egg mixture, slowly adding the remaining liqueur and juice between each addition. If the batter is too runny, stir in a couple of extra tablespoons of flour. Divide the batter between the muffin cups. Bake for 20–25 minutes until well risen. Remove from the oven. Transfer to a wire rack to cool completely.

Beat the cream cheese and sugar together, adding the food coloring. Pipe onto the cupcakes and decorate with the white sprinkles.

Store in an airtight container for up to 4 days, or freeze unfrosted for up to 3 months.

Makes 2 dozen

Cheeky Coffee Cupcakes

This unusual frosting only takes a couple of minutes to make. Once these cupcakes are frosted you can let them set or eat while they're still sticky—it's up to you!

For the cupcakes
3 extra-large eggs
¾ cup superfine sugar
1¼ cups all-purpose flour
2½ tsp. baking powder
¼ cup Dutch-process cocoa powder
¾ cup (1½ sticks) sweet butter
½ cup semisweet chocolate chips
1 tbsp. milk

For the frosting
4 oz white chocolate chips
2½ tbsp. cold black strong coffee
1 cup confectioners' sugar, sifted
2 tbsp. coffee liqueur
½ cup whipped heavy cream
3 tbsp. sifted cocoa, for dusting

TIP

Try a coffee-flavored buttercream frosting if you would like the cupcakes to last a day or two longer!

Preheat the oven to 350°F (175°C). Line two 12-cup muffin pans with paper baking cups.

Combine the cupcake ingredients in a large bowl and beat for 3–4 minutes with an electric mixer until smooth. Divide the mixture between the cups and bake for 15 minutes until well risen and golden brown. Remove from the oven and cool for 5 minutes. Transfer to a wire rack to cool completely.

To make the frosting, put the white chocolate chips and coffee in a double boiler and heat until melted. Remove from the heat and stir in the confectioners' sugar and coffee liqueur. Fold in the whipped cream. Spread the frosting over the cupcakes and sprinkle over the cocoa. Store in an airtight container for up to 2 days, or freeze unfrosted for up to 3 months.

Makes 2 dozen

Millionaire's Cupcakes

This is a delicious take on the classic chocolate and caramel slice. This caramel recipe is great to pour over any chocolatey cupcake base.

For the base
1 cup (2 sticks) sweet butter, softened
1 cup superfine sugar
2 cups all-purpose flour
2 tsp. baking powder
4 large eggs
1 tsp. vanilla extract

For the caramel
1 cup sweet butter
1 cup light brown sugar
2 x 14-oz cans condensed milk

For the chocolate
8 oz milk or semisweet chocolate, broken into pieces

TIP

You could drizzle the chocolate over the caramel for a different look.

Preheat the oven to 350°F (175°C). Place 24 paper baking cups in muffin pans.

Place all the ingredients for the base in a medium bowl and beat with an electric mixer until smooth and pale, about 2–3 minutes. Spoon the mixture into the cups to come just under half way up the sides. Bake for 10–15 minutes.

For the caramel, place the butter and brown sugar in a saucepan over a low heat until melted. Add the condensed milk and bring slowly to the boil. Stir continuously until the mixture turns a pale caramel color, approximately 3–4 minutes. Carefully pour over the top of the cupcakes and level with the back of a wooden spoon. Chill in the refrigerator for 1 hour, or until set.

Melt the chocolate in a bowl over a pan of simmering water and pipe over the caramel in a dollar sign shape. Chill in the refrigerator until set. Store in an airtight container for up to 3 days, or freeze unfrosted for up to 3 months.

Makes 2 dozen

Lacy Chocolate Cupcakes

Zig-zagging chocolate icing over cupcakes is great fun, and is a unique way to add sophistication and a lace-like effect to the cakes.

For the cupcakes
½ cup (1 stick) sweet butter
1 oz (2 tbsp.) sugar
2 extra-large eggs
1 tsp vanilla extract
½ cup (3½ oz) plain chocolate, finely grated
1 cup all-purpose flour
1½ tsp. baking powder
2 tablespoons cornflour

For the chocolate glaze
½ cup (3½ oz) white chocolate chips
½ cup (3½ oz) dark chocolate chips

TIP

Try writing letters with your chocolate, and use the cupcakes to spell out a (short!) message.

Preheat the oven to 350°F (175°C). Line 16 deep muffin or bun tins with paper cups.

Put the butter and sugar into a bowl and cream until light and fluffy. Beat the eggs a little at a time. Stir in the vanilla extract and chocolate. Then fold in the flours and baking powder.

Divide the mixture between the cases. Bake for about 15–20 minutes. Cool.

For the chocolate glaze, melt the white and the dark chocolate separately in double boilers, stirring until completely melted. Cool slightly, then using a skewer, zig-zag the dark chocolate over the cupcakes, then zig-zag over the white chocolate. Refrigerate until set.

Makes 16

Chai Cupcakes

Chai is a spiced Indian tea made with frothy warm milk—almost like an Indian cappuccino! This cupcake captures its light, spicy flavor.

For the cupcakes
2 cups all-purpose flour
1½ tsp. baking powder
pinch of salt
1 tbsp. Chai tea powder
¼ cup (½ stick) sweet butter, softened
¾ cup packed light brown sugar
2 extra-large egg whites
⅔ cup buttermilk

For the frosting
1 cup cream cheese, softened
1½ cups confectioners' sugar, sifted
1 tbsp. lemon juice
1 tsp. vanilla extract

TIP
You could try adding 2 teaspoons cinnamon to the dry ingredients, and 1 tablespoon grated orange zest along with the buttermilk.

Preheat the oven to 350°F (175°C). Place 12 baking cups in a muffin pan.

In a medium bowl, mix the flour, baking powder, salt, and Chai powder. In a separate bowl, beat the butter and sugar until smooth. Add the egg whites slowly, beating well. Slowly add the flour mixture, baking powder, and finally the buttermilk. Mix until combined. Spoon the batter into the cups. Bake for 20 minutes. Remove pan from the oven and cool for 5 minutes. Then remove the cupcakes and cool on a rack.

To make the frosting, mix the cream cheese and confectioners' sugar together in a medium bowl and beat until soft and light. Add the lemon and vanilla, and beat until smooth. Spoon the frosting over the cupcakes. Store unfrosted in an airtight container for up to 3 days, or freeze for up to 3 months.

Makes 1 dozen

Fennel & Pink Pepper Cupcakes

Lightly crushed fennel seeds give this cupcake a sweet licorice flavor. In India, fennel seeds are chewed after meals to refresh the breath.

TIP

You could add 1 tablespoon finely grated orange zest to the cupcake mixture.

For the cupcakes
1 cup (2 sticks) sweet butter, softened
1 cup superfine sugar
2 cups all-purpose flour
2½ tsp. baking powder
4 large eggs
1 tsp. finely crushed fennel seeds

For the frosting
1 cup cream cheese, softened
1½ cups confectioners' sugar, sifted
1 tsp. finely crushed pink peppercorns
1 tsp. lightly crushed fennel seeds

Preheat the oven to 350°F (175°C). Place 18 paper baking cups in muffin pans.

Combine all the cupcake ingredients in a medium bowl and beat with an electric mixer until smooth and pale, about 2–3 minutes. Spoon the batter into the cups. Bake for 20 minutes. Remove pans from the oven and cool for 5 minutes. Then remove the cupcakes and cool on a rack.

To make the frosting, combine the cream cheese and confectioners' sugar, and beat briskly until soft and creamy. Add the pink peppercorns, and stir well. Swirl onto the top of the cupcakes, and decorate with the fennel seeds.

Store unfrosted for up to 3 days in an airtight container, or freeze for 3 months.

Makes 1½ dozen

Fig & Hazelnut Cupcakes

Sweet, nutty, and rich with the intense flavor of fig, these cupcakes are perfect for any occasion. Bake them when you have guests for coffee, or just enjoy them as an everyday treat.

⅔ cup roasted hazelnuts
¾ cup (1½ sticks) sweet butter, at room temperature
½ cup superfine sugar
¼ cup light brown sugar

2 extra-large eggs
finely grated zest of 1 lemon
scant 1¼ cups all-purpose flour
1 tsp. baking powder
⅔ cup dried figs, chopped

TIP

This can be easily adapted to make date, apricot, or raisin and hazelnut cupcakes.

Preheat the oven to 350°F (175°C). Line two 12-cup muffin pans with paper baking cups.

Put the hazelnuts in a food processor and process until coarsely ground, then set aside. Beat together the butter and sugars until smooth and creamy, then beat in the eggs one at a time. Stir in the lemon zest, then sift the flour and baking powder over the batter. Add the ground nuts and fold together until well mixed. Fold in the figs.

Divide the mixture between the cups. Bake for 20–25 minutes until well risen and golden brown. Remove from the oven and cool for 5 minutes. Transfer to a wire rack to cool completely.

Store in an airtight container for up to 4 days, or freeze unfrosted for up to 3 months.

Makes 2 dozen

Couscous Cupcakes

Couscous, the world's smallest pasta, is a staple throughout northern Africa. It gives these cakes a light and elegant texture.

½ cup couscous
½ cup boiling water
2 cups all-purpose flour
2 tbsp. superfine sugar
1 tbsp. baking powder
pinch of salt

1 tsp. toasted cumin seeds
1 tsp. ground coriander
1 extra-large egg
4 tbsp. olive oil
1 tbsp. lemon zest
2 tbsp. chopped flat-leaf parsley

TIP

Vary the spice mix for variations—try chili powder, tumeric, or even saffron.

Preheat the oven to 350°F (175°C). Place 24 mini paper cups in a muffin pan.

Put the couscous in a medium bowl and pour the boiling water over it. Cover and leave for 5 minutes, so the grains absorb the liquid. Fluff the grains apart with a fork.

Mix the dry ingredients in a bowl with a spoon. Beat the egg and oil in a large bowl with an electric mixer until combined. Add the couscous and the dry ingredients and mix until nearly combined. Fold in the lemon zest and parsley. Spoon the mixture into the cups. Bake for 20 minutes. Remove pan from the oven and cool for 5 minutes. Then remove the mini cakes and cool on a rack.

Store in an airtight container for up to 3 days, or freeze for up to 3 months.

Makes 2 dozen

Ginger Cupcakes with Whisky Syrup

All the flavor of a highball in a cupcake! This may seem like an unusual combination, but try it, and you'll want to make them again and again.

For the cupcakes
2 cups all-purpose flour
1 tbsp. baking powder
4 tsp. ground ginger
1 tsp. cinnamon
1 cup packed unrefined brown sugar
2 extra-large eggs
½ cup honey
½ cup (1 stick) butter, melted
¾ cup milk

2 tbsp. roughly chopped candied
  ginger

For the syrup
5 tbsp. light corn syrup
2 tbsp. whisky
2 tbsp. chopped walnuts or pecans

Preheat the oven to 350°F (175°C). Place 12 paper cups in a muffin pan.

Sift the flour, baking powder, ginger, and cinnamon into a large bowl. In a medium bowl combine the remaining ingredients for the cupcakes and beat with an electric mixer until smooth, about 2–3 minutes. Stir into the dry ingredients. Spoon the batter into the cups.

Bake for 20–25 minutes. Remove the pan from the oven and pierce the top of each cupcake a few times with a small skewer. Cool on a rack while you make the syrup.

For the syrup, heat the syrup and whisky together in a small pan. Stir in the chopped nuts, then drizzle over the cupcakes while they're still warm.

Store in an airtight container for up to 4 days, or freeze for up to 3 months.

Piña Colada Cupcakes

Everyone's favorite summer cocktail in a cupcake—what's not to love! A great cupcake to make if your summer vacation seems a long way off.

For the cupcakes
½ cup (3½ oz) canned pineapple
3 tbsp. Malibu
1 cup (2 sticks) sweet butter, softened
1 cup superfine sugar
2 cups all-purpose flour
2 tsp. baking powder
4 large eggs

For the topping
¼ cup (2½ oz) dessicated coconut
½ cup lightly whipped heavy cream
5 tbsp. Malibu
2 tbsp. demerara sugar

Preheat the oven to 350˚F (175˚C). Place 18 paper baking cups in muffin pans.

Combine all the cupcake ingredients in a large bowl and beat with an electric mixer until smooth and pale, about 2–3 minutes. Spoon the batter into the cups. Bake for 20 minutes. Cool on a rack.

Gently fold the coconut into the cream with the Malibu. Spoon over the cooled cupcakes, then sprinkle over the sugar.

Makes 1½ **dozen**

Cosmopolitan Cupcakes

The tartness of the cranberries is a deliciously sophisticated counterpoint to the sweet cupcake.

For the cupcakes
4 tbsp. vodka
1 cup fresh cranberries
zest and juice of 1 lime
1 cup (2 sticks) sweet butter, softened
1 cup superfine sugar
2 cups all-purpose flour
2 tsp. baking powder
4 large eggs

For the frosting
1 cup cream cheese, softened
1½ cups confectioners' sugar, sifted

To decorate
1 extra-large egg white
½ cup fresh cranberries
3 tbsp. superfine sugar
zest and juice of 1 lime

TIP

For more frosting options with fruit or petals, see page 234.

Preheat the oven to 350°F (175°C). Place 18 paper baking cups in muffin pans.

Gently heat the vodka, cranberries, and lime juice in a pan until hot, then bubble for 1–2 minutes. Remove from the heat and let cool. Combine the butter, sugar, flour, baking powder, and eggs in a medium bowl. Beat with an electric mixer until light and creamy, about 2–3 minutes. Stir in the cranberry mixture. Bake for 20 minutes. Remove pans from the oven and cool for 5 minutes. Then remove the cupcakes and cool on a rack.

To make the frosting, beat the cream cheese with the confectioners' sugar with an electric whisk until light and creamy. Gently beat in the lime zest and juice then spoon the frosting over the cupcakes.

To decorate, lightly whisk the egg white until frothy. Gently dip in a cranberry then roll it in the sugar to lightly coat all over. Put onto a sheet of baking parchment. Repeat with remaining cranberries. Arrange the frosted cranberries over the cupcakes with the zest.

Store in an airtight container for up to 4 days, or freeze for up to 3 months.

Makes 1½ dozen

Spiced Pumpkin & Sage Cupcakes

These savory tuiles are incredibly simple to make and will make these lightly spiced cupcakes look really special.

For the cupcakes
1 tbsp. olive oil
1 tbsp. chopped fresh sage
1 tsp. dried crushed chilies
4 cups all-purpose flour
2¼ cups cornmeal
1 tbsp. baking powder
pinch of salt
2 extra-large lightly beaten eggs
1½ cups (3 sticks) sweet butter, melted

1⅓ cups buttermilk
½ cup puréed pumpkin
4 tbsp. finely grated Parmesan cheese

For the tuiles
½ cup finely grated Parmesan cheese

For the topping
½ cup cream cheese
1 tsp. freshly ground black pepper

TIP
Sweet tuiles can also be made with flour, eggs, butter, and sugar.

Preheat the oven to 350°F (175°C). Place 12 paper baking cups in a muffin pan. Heat the oil in a pan and fry the sage and crushed chili for 2–3 minutes until softened. Remove from the pan and allow to cool.

In a medium bowl, mix the flour, cornmeal, baking powder, and salt. In a large bowl, beat the eggs, butter, and buttermilk until combined. Stir in the sage mixture, pumpkin, and 2 tablespoons Parmesan, then stir in the flour mixture until just combined. Spoon the mixture into the prepared pan. Top with the remaining Parmesan. Bake for 25–30 minutes. Remove pan from the oven—leave the oven on—and cool.

To make the tuiles, divide the Parmesan into 12 small balls and spread out over two flat cookie sheets (make sure they are spaced well apart as they will spread during cooking—bake them in two batches if you only have one cookie sheet). Bake in the preheated oven for 8–10 minutes until the cheese is melted and lightly golden. Remove from the oven and lift the tuiles from the baking sheet with a palate knife (it's much easier to remove them while they're still hot). Drape the tuiles over a rolling pin to cool and harden, taking them off as they set to make room for others. Beat the cream cheese with the black pepper. Dot over the cooled cupcakes, then top each with a tuile.

Makes 1 dozen

Dessert Cupcakes

Based on popular desserts these cupcakes are intended to be served as such—some can be served warm, à la mode, others with sauce on the side. Favorites such as Tiramisu, Sticky Toffee Pudding, Crumble, and Lemon Meringue are featured.

Dessert Cupcakes

Dessert cupcakes are about indulging your sweet tooth, so don't be afraid to try any new ideas that tickle your fancy. Whether it's switching frostings or playing with different kinds of chocolate chips, these reliable recipes will stand up to a little tinkering. Always make the main recipe at least once before trying alterations.

You may want to tailor your delicious dessert cupcakes for a certain occasion or season. A warm orange recipe might be mouthwatering in winter, but what about the summer months? It's easy to substitute orange zest with lemon or lime to get that seasonal taste change. Similarly, if you're not a walnut fan, try pecans or macadamia nuts. They vary in price, but it's up to you to create the flavors you're nuts about!

If a recipe calls for soft caramels, you may want to use the chocolate-coated variety. This will give your dessert cupcake that extra decadent twist that the whole family will love. Alternatively, toning down the sugar content is simple with sugar-substitute and bittersweet chocolate. This is a general rule that works for cupcake batter, but not for sauces and syrups. If you're trying to go low-carb, it might be better to use store-bought, sugar-free accompaniments.

Warm Orange Cupcakes

These warm, delicate cupcakes make a perfect accompaniment to a winter salad of dried fruits. Or serve with curd (see page 22), fresh whipped cream, or crème fraîche for a brunch, snack dessert, or treat.

1¼ cups all-purpose flour
2 tsp. baking powder
½ tsp. salt
½ cup superfine sugar
1 medium eating orange, peeled,
    and segmented

1 extra-large egg
grated zest of 1 orange
½ tsp vanilla extract
1 cup buttermilk
½ stick butter, melted and cooled

TIP

For a sweet treat, try piercing the top of each cupcake and drizzling with a syrup made from orange juice and sugar.

Preheat the oven to 400˚F (200˚C). Grease or spray a 12-cup muffin pan or line with paper cups. Sift the flour, baking powder, and salt into a large bowl, then stir in the sugar and chopped orange peel, and make a well in the center.

Beat the egg, orange zest, and vanilla extract in another bowl until foamy. Beat in the buttermilk, and melted butter. Pour into the well, and lightly stir until just combined. Do not over-mix; the batter should be slightly lumpy.

Spoon the batter into the prepared cups, filling each about ¾ full. Bake for 20 minutes until risen and golden. Remove pan to a wire rack to cool, about 2 minutes, then remove cupcakes to the rack to cool.

Store in an airtight container for up to 3 days or freeze for up to 3 months.

Makes 1 dozen

Ginger & Caramel Cupcakes

A spicy, gooey mix, ginger and caramel cupcakes are a real indulgence and are delicious served with hot custard.

½ cup (1 stick) sweet butter, softened
¾ cup packed brown sugar
2 extra-large lightly beaten eggs
2 tbsp. instant coffee granules
1 tbsp. boiling water

2⅔ cups all-purpose flour
3½ tsp. baking powder
½ cup milk
3 tbsp. chopped candied ginger
½ cup (3½ oz) soft caramels

Preheat the oven to 350˚F (175˚C). Place 12 paper baking cups in a muffin pan.

In a medium bowl, beat the butter and sugar until pale and creamy. Add the eggs slowly. In a small bowl, dissolve the coffee in the water. Beat the coffee into the butter mixture. Add the flour, baking powder, and milk, and beat until well combined. Stir in the candied ginger.

Spoon the mixture into the cups. Push a couple of the caramels into the center of each cupcake, and place them in the oven. Bake for 20 minutes. Cool for 5 minutes in the pan. Turn onto a plate and serve while warm.

Store in an airtight container for up to 2 days.

Makes 1 dozen

TIP

Try substituting the coffee granules with 1½ teaspoons ground ginger added to the batter for a really spicy treat.

Sticky Toffee & Walnut Pudding Cupcakes

This is an old classic British pudding that has recently enjoyed a bit of a renaissance.

For the cupcakes
1½ cups all-purpose flour
2 tsp. baking powder
⅔ cup packed brown sugar
½ cup milk
1 extra-large egg
1 tsp. vanilla extract
3 tbsp. sweet butter, melted

½ cup (3½ oz) chopped dates
⅔ cup (4 oz) chopped walnuts

For the topping
½ cup packed brown sugar
4 tbsp. sweet butter
⅔ cup boiling water
8 walnut halves, to serve

TIP
Replace the walnuts with pecans both in the batter and for the topping.

Preheat the oven to 375˚F (190˚C). Line 8 muffin pans with baking parchment.

In a medium bowl, combine the flour, baking powder, and sugar. In a separate medium bowl beat the milk, egg, vanilla, and butter until smooth and pale, about 2–3 minutes. Pour the batter over the flour mixture and stir with a wooden spoon. Fold in the dates and walnuts. Spoon the mixture into the muffin pans, filling each cup about halfway. For the topping, sprinkle 1 tablespoon of the sugar on top of the batter in each cup. Add ½ tablespoon butter, then pour about 1 tablespoon water over each.

Bake for 25 minutes. Remove from oven and cool for 5 minutes in the pan. Invert onto plates, peel off the parchment, and decorate with walnut halves. Serve immediately.

Makes 8

Mini Raspberry & Coconut Cupcakes

The inspiration for these cupcakes came from the classic English Bakewell tart. Serve with crème anglaise or cream.

3 tbsp. ground almond
½ cup (2½ oz) flaked coconut
1½ cups confectioners' sugar, sifted
1½ cups all-purpose flour
1 tsp. baking powder
½ cup (1 stick) sweet butter, melted

5 large egg whites
2 cups fresh or thawed, frozen raspberries
2 tbsp. shredded coconut

TIP

This recipe is inspired by the classic English Bakewell tart, so feel free to replace the flaked and shredded coconut with almonds.

Preheat the oven to 375°F (190°C). Place 24 mini ceramic baking cups on a cookie sheet.

In a large bowl, combine the ground almond, coconut, confectioners' sugar, flour, and baking powder. Stir in the butter, followed by the egg whites. Spoon the mixture into the cups. Drop a raspberry and some of the shredded coconut on top of each cupcake. Bake for 12–15 minutes. Remove the cups from the oven and cool for 5 minutes. Then remove the cupcakes and cool on a rack.

Store in an airtight container for up to 2 days, or freeze in sealed containers for up to 3 months.

Makes 2 dozen

Rhubarb & Custard Cupcakes

The combination of rhubarb and ginger is magnificent. It is believed that rhubarb originated in China, where it was used for its medicinal properties.

1 cup (2 sticks) sweet butter, softened
1 cup superfine sugar
2 cups all-purpose flour
3 tsp. baking powder
4 large eggs
1 tsp. vanilla extract

1 cup cooked rhubarb
1½ cups readymade vanilla custard (or see page 242 for a vanilla custard recipe)

Preheat the oven to 400˚F (200˚C). Place 18 paper baking cups in muffin pans.

Combine all the cupcake ingredients, except the rhubarb, in a medium bowl and beat with an electric mixer until smooth and pale, about 2–3 minutes. Stir in the rhubarb and spoon the batter into the cups. Bake for 20 minutes. Remove pans from the oven and cool for 5 minutes. Then remove the cupcakes and cool on a rack. Serve with custard.

Store unfrosted in an airtight container for up to 3 days, or freeze for up to 3 months.

Makes 1½ **dozen**

Chocolate Soufflé Cupcakes

Rich and light at the same time, soufflé makes a wonderfully indulgent dessert at any dinner party.

For the cupcakes
melted sweet butter to butter
   the dishes
sugar for the dishes
3½ tbsp. soft sweet butter
½ cup all-purpose flour
½ tsp. baking powder
1 cup milk

¼ cup chocolate couverture,
   chopped
4 large eggs
⅓ cup superfine sugar
pinch of salt

To decorate
confectioners' sugar

TIP

Try dusting with cocoa powder instead of confectioners' sugar for a more sophisticated finish.

Preheat the oven to 400°F (200°C).

Butter 8 soufflé dishes or cups evenly with cooled (almost cold) melted butter and sprinkle with sugar. The base and sides of the dishes must be completely covered. Tip out the excess sugar.

Separate the eggs. Knead together the butter, flour, and baking powder. Put the milk into a pan, add the chopped chocolate couverture and sugar and bring to a boil, stirring. Break the flour and butter mixture into pieces and stir into the boiling milk one at a time, stirring until the flour has bound with the liquid and formed a homogenous mass. Let cool to lukewarm, then whisk in the egg yolks one at a time, whisking until the mixture is smooth and creamy again. Beat the egg whites with a pinch of salt until they form soft peaks.

Stir about ¼ of the beaten egg white into the soufflé mixture with the whisk, to lighten the mixture. Then fold in the rest of the beaten egg with a wooden spoon. Fill the prepared dishes or cups with the mixture to about half an inch below the rim. Place the dishes in a baking dish and add boiling water to a depth of about ¾ inch below the rim of the dishes. Bake for 25–30 minutes. Take out of the oven. Place a paper heart on top of each soufflé and sprinkle with confectioners' sugar. Remove the paper heart and serve immediately.

Makes 8

Chocolate Ice Cream Cupcakes

It's best to move these cupcakes from freezer to refrigerator 30 minutes before serving.

For the cupcakes
1 cup (2 sticks) sweet butter, softened
1 cup superfine sugar
1½ cups all-purpose flour
4 tbsp. Dutch-process cocoa powder
1 tsp. baking powder
4 large eggs
1 tsp. vanilla extract

For the filling and glaze
1 cup chocolate ice cream
½ cup (3½ oz) semisweet chocolate chips
⅓ cup heavy cream

Preheat the oven to 350°F (175°C). Place 18 paper baking cups in muffin pans.

Combine all the cupcake ingredients in a medium bowl and beat with an electric mixer until smooth and creamy, about 2–3 minutes.

Spoon the batter into the cups. Bake for 20 minutes. Remove pans from the oven and cool for 5 minutes. Then remove the cupcakes and cool on a rack. When cool, slice the cupcakes horizontally and spread a little softened ice cream on the bottom slice. Place the top back on the cupcake and freeze.

Prepare the glaze by melting the chocolate in a double boiler or a medium bowl over a pan of simmering water, stirring until completely melted. Remove from the heat. Add the cream and stir until well combined. Cool slightly and spoon over the cupcakes. Return to the freezer to set. Freeze in an airtight container for up to 3 months.

Makes 1½ dozen

Mixed Berry Crumble Cupcakes

These crumbly-topped cupcakes hide a sweet surprise. Serve them right out of the oven, with custard (see page 242).

For the filling
2½ cups mixed berries (blackberries, strawberries, raspberries)
3 tbsp. superfine sugar
2 tbsp. water
¼ tsp. lemon zest

For the crumble
2 tbsp. sweet butter, melted
4 tbsp. all-purpose flour
3 tbsp. light brown sugar

4 tbsp. rolled oats
1 tsp. lemon zest

For the cupcakes
3 cups all-purpose flour
¾ cup packed brown sugar
pinch of salt
2 tsp. baking powder
½ cup (1 stick) sweet butter, melted
1¼ cups milk
1 extra-large egg

Preheat the oven to 400°F (200°C). Grease a 12-cup muffin pan.

Combine all the filling ingredients in a small saucepan. Gently bring to a simmer, and cook for 5 minutes, until the berries give some of their juices. Set aside.

Stir all the crumble ingredients in a small bowl and set aside. For the cupcakes, combine the dry ingredients in a large bowl. In a medium bowl, beat the butter, milk, and egg. Add the egg mixture to the dry ingredients and stir until just combined. Using about half the batter, spoon a little batter into each cup, then spoon a layer of the filling.

Add the remaining batter, and top with the crumble mixture. Bake for 20 minutes. Remove pan from the oven and cool for 5 minutes. Serve cupcakes warm, with custard if desired.

Store in an airtight container for up to 3 days, or freeze for up to 3 months.

Makes 1 dozen

Caramelized Banana Split Cupcakes

These caramelized banana split cupcakes are creamy and delicious. They will satisfy the most severe dessert craving!

For the cupcakes
1 cup (2 sticks) sweet butter, softened
1 cup superfine sugar
2 cups all-purpose flour
3 tsp. baking powder
4 large eggs
1 tsp. vanilla extract

For the caramelized bananas
3 tbsp. unsalted butter
3 tbsp. superfine sugar
2 bananas, each cut into 9 discs about 1-in thick
2 tbsp. store-bought caramel sauce
½ cup whipped heavy cream

TIP
For a fun take on this classic dessert, try serving sprinkled with chocolate chips!

Preheat the oven to 350°F (175°C). Place 18 paper baking cups in muffin pans.

Place all the cupcake ingredients in a medium bowl and beat with an electric mixer until smooth and pale, about 2–3 minutes. Spoon the mixture into the cups. Bake for 20 minutes.

Remove the pans from the oven and cool for 5 minutes, then remove the cupcakes and cool on a rack.

Meanwhile, melt the butter in a large skillet. Sprinkle over the sugar and leave to cook for 3–4 minutes until lightly golden. Add the bananas, cut-side down, and cook gently for 5 minutes until golden and caramelized underneath. Carefully turn with a palate knife and cook for 5 minutes on the other side until golden all over. Remove from the pan and set aside.

Stir the caramel sauce into the whipped cream, then pipe or spoon onto the top of the cupcakes and top each with a piece of caramelized banana.

Store without the bananas and cream in an airtight container for up to 3 days, or freeze for up to 3 months.

Makes 1½ dozen

Tiramisu Cupcakes

Use the best quality coffee you can for these cupcakes—the coffee is where most of the flavor is.

TIP

Serve with a fresh cream for a really indulgent dessert.

For the cupcakes
3 extra-large eggs
¾ cup superfine sugar
1¼ cups all-purpose flour
1½ tsp. baking powder
¼ cup Dutch-process cocoa
    powder
¾ cup (1½ sticks) sweet butter
½ cup semisweet chocolate chips
1 tbsp. milk
5 tbsp. cold espresso or strong
    black coffee

For the filling
1 cup mascarpone
1 tsp. vanilla extract
¼ cup confectioners' sugar, sifted
2 tbsp. Dutch process cocoa, sifted

Preheat the oven to 350°F (175°C). Line 2 12-cup muffin pans with paper baking cups.

Combine the cupcake ingredients except for the espresso in a large bowl and beat for 3–4 minutes with an electric mixer until smooth. Divide the mixture between the cups and bake for 15 minutes until well risen and golden brown. Remove the pan from the oven and pierce the top of each cupcake a few times with a small skewer. Pour over half the espresso, then leave to cool completely.

Meanwhile, beat the mascarpone with the vanilla extract, remaining espresso, and sugar in a bowl. Slice the cooled cupcakes in half horizontally, then spoon a little mascarpone mixture onto the base. Pop the tops back on, then spoon over the remaining mascarpone mixture, pressing down at the edges with a spoon. Dust with cocoa.

Store in the refrigerator for up to one day or without the mascarpone mixture in an airtight container for up to 4 days.

Makes 2 dozen

Creamy Summer Pudding Cupcakes

This is a great way of using up leftover bread. Traditionally, berries are used, but you can use any juicy fruit: peeled, chopped citrus fruits are equally delicious!

12 slices white bread, crusts
   removed
1½ cups mixed frozen berries,
   such as blueberries, raspberries,
   strawberries
6 tbsp. fruit juice (fresh or reserved
   from the frozen fruit)

3 tbsp. fruit liqueur, such as
   strawberry or raspberry (optional)

To decorate
1 cup whipped heavy cream
½ cup fresh berries
2–3 tbsp. confectioners' sugar

TIP

These no-cook cupcakes taste better the day after they are made.

Use a cookie cutter to cut each slice of bread into 2 discs to fit into the base of a muffin pan.

Pour over 2–3 tablespoons reserved fruit juice, then spoon over half the fruit. Top with another bread disc, then repeat with the juice and remaining fruit. Drizzle over the fruit liqueur, and leave for at least an hour (preferably overnight).

Whip the cream to soft peaks, and spoon over the cakes. Decorate with fresh berries and dust with confectioners' sugar.

Makes 1 dozen

Tropical Trifle Cupcakes

These are refreshing enough to end with after a hearty meal.

For the cupcakes
½ cup (1 stick) of butter
3 tbsp. creamed coconut, at room temperature
¾ cup superfine sugar
3 extra-large eggs
1 cup all-purpose flour
1½ tsp. baking powder
scant ⅔ cup shredded coconut

For the topping
1 cup whipping cream
12 strawberries. halved
12 grapes, halved
½ star fruit, pitted, peeled, and sliced
8-oz can pineapple chunks

Preheat the oven to 350°F (175°C). Line two 12-cup muffin pans with paper baking cups.

Beat together the butter, creamed coconut, and sugar until pale and creamy. Beat in the eggs, one at a time. Sift the flour and baking powder over the bowl, then fold in. Stir in the shredded coconut. Spoon the batter into the prepared pans and spread out evenly using the back of the spoon. Bake for 15–20 minutes until golden brown and a skewer inserted in the center comes out clean. Turn the cupcakes out onto a wire rack and let cool completely.

Just before serving, whip the cream. Spread over the cupcakes. Top with the strawberries, grapes, star fruit, and pineapple chunks.

Makes 2 dozen

Pear and Bittersweet Chocolate Cupcakes

Pears are packed full of vitamins. They have high levels of vitamin A and beta carotene which help keep the immune system strong and combat the signs of aging.

For the cupcakes
2 cups drained stewed or canned pears
1½ cups all-purpose flour
¾ cup whole wheat flour
2 tsp. baking powder

pinch of salt
⅓ cup packed brown sugar
1 extra-large lightly beaten egg
4 tbsp. vegetable oil
½ cup whole milk
3 fresh pears

For the ganache
1 cup heavy cream
8 oz semisweet chocolate, broken into small pieces

Preheat the oven to 350°F (175°C). Line a 12-cup muffin pan with paper baking cups. Purée the pears in a food processor. In a medium bowl, combine the flours, baking powder, salt, and sugar with a spoon.

In a large bowl, beat the egg, oil, and milk with an electric mixer until combined. Stir in the pear puree, then add the flour mixture and baking powder, and mix until combined. Spoon the mixture into the cups. Add the 3 fresh pears, quartered and laid over the top. Bake for 20 minutes. Remove pan from the oven and cool for 5 minutes. Then remove the cupcakes and cool on a rack.

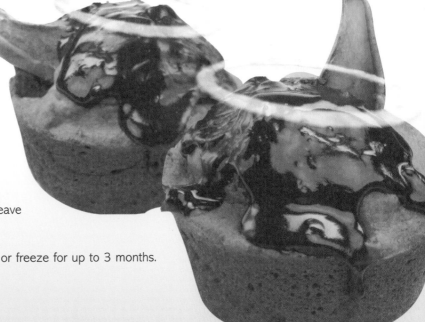

Heat the cream to just below boiling. Remove from the heat. Add the chocolate. Leave for several minutes to melt, then beat well. Leave to cool. Spoon evenly over the cupcakes and leave to set.

Store in an airtight container for up to 3 days, or freeze for up to 3 months.

Makes 1 dozen

Baked Alaska Cupcakes

Frozen, not fresh, berries are essential for this recipe—don't thaw them first as they'll soften in heat of the oven.

For the cupcakes
1 cup (2 sticks) sweet
   butter, softened
1 cup superfine sugar
2 cups all-purpose
   flour
3 tsp. baking powder
4 large eggs
1 tsp. vanilla extract

For the filling
⅓ cup mixed frozen
   berries (no
   need to thaw first)
1 cup vanilla ice cream

For the meringue
3 extra-large
   egg whites
¼ tsp. cream of tartar
⅓ cup granulated
sugar

Preheat the oven to 350˚F (175˚C). Place 18 paper baking cups in muffin pans.

Place all the cupcake ingredients in a large bowl, and beat with an electric mixer until smooth and pale, about 2–3 minutes. Spoon the batter into the cups. Bake for 20 minutes. Remove pans from the oven and cool for 5 minutes. Then remove the cupcakes and cool on a rack.

For the filling, combine the ice cream with berries with their juice in a small bowl. Remove the top from each cupcake and hollow out a small hole. Spoon the ice cream filling into the hole and replace the top. Loosely cover the trays, then put into the freezer while you make the meringue.

Beat the eggs and cream of tartar until soft peaks form. Add one-third of the sugar and beat for 1 minute. Repeat until all the sugar has been added. Increase the oven temperature to 450˚F (230˚C). Spoon or pipe the meringue on top of the cupcakes.

Bake for 5 minutes until the meringue is golden. Serve immediately.

Makes 1½ dozen

Double Chocolate Mousse Cupcakes

As the quantities are generous and the mousse is very rich, you could divide the mixture into 18 and serve in mini-muffin cups.

6 oz white chocolate
1 tbsp. Cointreau liqueur
2½ tbsp. water
1¼ cups whipping cream
1 cup (4 oz) semisweet
 chocolate chips

2 extra-large eggs, separated
chocolate leaves, to decorate
fresh mint leaves, to decorate

TIP

Try serving with fresh raspberries instead of mint leaves.

Place 12 paper baking cups in muffin pans. Put the white chocolate, liqueur, and water in a double boiler and heat. Beat the cream with an electric mixer until soft peaks form. Fold into the white chocolate mixture. Divide the mixture between the cups (to come halfway up the sides) and refrigerate for 2 hours.

Melt the semisweet chocolate in a double boiler. Remove from the heat, cool a little, then stir in the egg yolks. Beat the egg whites in a medium bowl with an electric mixer, until stiff peaks form. Fold into the melted chocolate. Pour the chocolate mixture on top of the white mousse and chill for 3–4 hours.

Decorate with chocolate leaves and fresh mint leaves and serve.

Makes 1 dozen

Apple & Cinnamon Cupcakes

Cinnamon brings a delicate sweetness to this cupcake recipe and complements the applesauce marvelously.

½ cup (1 stick) sweet butter, softened
½ cup plus 1 tbsp. superfine sugar
1 cup all-purpose flour
1½ tsp. baking powder
2 extra-large eggs
¾ cup unsweetened applesauce
¾ tsp. cinnamon

½ cup (3½ oz) chopped pecans
½ cup (3½ oz) golden raisins
1 small red eating apple, thinly sliced
2 tbsp. granulated sugar
vanilla custard, to serve (see page 242)

TIP

These are delicious served with vanilla custard (page 242).

Preheat the oven to 350°F (175°C). Place 12 paper baking cups in a muffin pan.

Place the butter, sugar, flour, baking powder, and egg in a bowl and beat with an electric mixer until smooth and pale, about 2–3 minutes. Stir in the applesauce, cinnamon, pecans, and raisins. Spoon the batter into the cups. Lay the apple slices on top and sprinkle with a little sugar.

Bake for 25 minutes. Remove pan from the oven and cool for 5 minutes. Then remove the cupcakes and cool for 1 minute on a rack. Serve warm with custard.

Store in an airtight container for up to 3 days, or freeze for up to 3 months.

Makes 1 dozen

Praline Truffle Cupcakes

When making the praline, keep an eye on the sugar as it cooks and browns very quickly.

½ cup superfine sugar
1 cup whole blanched almonds
3 cups (1 lb. 2 oz) semisweet
   chocolate
1½ cups whipping cream
⅔ cup (1⅓ sticks) sweet butter
1 tbsp. rum
confectioners' sugar to dust

Lightly grease 18 muffin pan cups. Grease a cookie sheet.

Put the sugar and almonds in a small saucepan and cook over a low heat until the sugar has melted. Cook for 1 minute until it turns a pale golden brown. Pour the almond praline onto the cookie sheet and allow to cool completely.

Melt all but 4 oz of the chocolate in a double boiler. Remove from heat and leave to cool. Put the praline in a plastic food bag and crush with a rolling pin. Whisk the cream with an electric mixer until soft peaks form.

In a separate bowl, beat the butter until light and then add the cooled chocolate and rum and beat to combine. Fold in the whipped cream and praline then spoon the mixture into the prepared pans. Leave to set for 3–4 hours, or overnight.

Melt the remaining chocolate and spread onto a parchment paper-lined cookie sheet. Allow to set completely. Using a sharp knife, draw the blade at an angle across the chocolate to form curls and ruffles. Run a warm knife around the edge of the muffin cups and invert the cakes onto serving plates. Pile the chocolate curls on top, dust lightly with confectioners' sugar, and serve.

Makes 1½ **dozen**

Frostings & Decoration

A selection of frosting, decoration, and sauce
recipes, including flavor adaptations and
serving suggestions for your saintly cupcakes.

Basic Glaze

This is a simple way to add an attractive shine to your cupcakes if you're not going to frost them.

¾ cup (8 oz) apricot jelly
2 tbsp. water
squeeze lemon juice

Place the jelly, water, and lemon juice in a small saucepan. Heat gently until the jelly has dissolved. Then boil for 1 minute. Strain and cool. Brush over the top of cooled cupcakes to glaze.

TIP

This glaze is useful for attaching decorations, such as chopped nuts, fruit, or leaves. Just press them onto the glaze before it cools.

Sprinkles & Candies

The easiest way to decorate a cupcake is by topping frosting or a glaze with sprinkles or candies. There is a fine array around, from chocolate chips to jelly beans.

Classic Buttercream

You can flavor this buttercream with vanilla extract or finely grated lemon or orange zest.

½ cup (1 stick) sweet butter, at
   room temperature
2 cups confectioners' sugar

Beat the butter until light and fluffy, then beat in the confectioners' sugar, a little at a time, until well mixed. Spread over the cupcakes, or store in an airtight container in the refrigerator.

TIP

If you're making the frosting in advance, bring it to room temperature first before spreading on a cupcake.

Ready-to-roll Fondant Sheet

This fondant requires no cooking and keeps for weeks.

4 cups confectioners' sugar
1 egg white
2 tbsp. liquid glucose, warmed

Place most of the sugar in a bowl. Make a well in the center and add the egg white and glucose. Beat the mixture with a wooden spoon, or work it with your hands to make a firm paste, adding extra sugar as required. Place fondant on a work surface lightly sprinkled with confectioners' sugar and knead lightly. Store in an airtight container in the refrigerator for several weeks.

Marzipan

You can buy ready-made marzipan, but it's easy to make.

2½ cups ground almonds
½ cup superfine sugar
1 large beaten egg
1 tbsp. lemon juice

Combine the almonds and sugar together, then add the egg and lemon juice. Stir together well, tip out onto a clean work surface, knead until smooth, then wrap in plastic wrap until ready to use.

Frosted Fruit & Petals

This works well with petals, leaves, berries, or herbs to decorate sweet cupcakes.

1 extra-large egg white
¼ cup superfine sugar
selection of clean petals, leaves
    berries, or herbs

Gently whisk the egg white in a bowl with a fork until foamy. Gently brush over the petals, berries, or herbs on both sides. Sprinkle with the sugar until evenly coated and shake off any excess. Place on a sheet of non-stick paper on a baking sheet and leave to dry in a warm place. Remove carefully and store in an airtight tin, between layers of tissue paper.

TIP

For safety precautions, prepare the frosted decorations on the same day they are to be consumed.

Ganache

A ganache is a rich chocolate frosting made from melted chocolate and heavy cream. It can be flavored with liqueur, spirits, or extracts.

1 cup heavy cream
1 cup (8 oz) plain chocolate, broken
   into small pieces

Heat the cream to just below boiling. Remove from the heat. Add the chocolate. Leave for several minutes to melt, then beat well. Let cool. If wished, whip the ganache until pale and doubled in bulk. If wished, flavor with a splash of liqueur or spirit, or a few drops of vanilla or orange extract. Spoon evenly over the cupcakes and leave to set.

TIP

If wished, you could whip the ganache until pale and doubled in bulk.

Chocolate Frosting

This is a spreadable icing that is quick to make and easy use.

½ cup (4 oz.) plain or milk
  chocolate
2 tbsp. unsalted butter
5 tbsp. milk
2 cups confectioners' sugar

Melt the chocolate and butter in a saucepan with the milk over a gentle heat. Add the confectioners' sugar and beat well. Allow to cool, then swirl over the cupcakes with a small palate knife or spoon.

Chocolate Decorations

Chocolate can complement the flavors of a chocolate cupcake and can contrast very effectively with fruity flavors. These ideas can really vamp up delicious cupcakes whether you are serving as a dessert or a special treat.

Chocolate shapes
Pour melted chocolate onto a sheet of parchment paper and use a palette knife to spread it out to 1½-inch thickness. Let cool until the chocolate becomes cloudy but has not set. Dip a cookie cutter in hot water and use to stamp out chocolate shapes. Let the shapes set on a separate sheet of parchment paper.

Chocolate curls
Hold a block of room-temperature white or unsweetened chocolate and run a vegetable peeler up and down one side to make curls. The cheaper the chocolate the better it tends to curl.

Crème au Beurre

This is a deliciously rich buttercream. You can flavor it with a few drops of extract, finely grated zest of orange and lemon, or color it with food coloring.

scant ½ cup granulated sugar
4 tbsp. water
2 extra-large egg yolks
¾ cup unsalted butter

Place the sugar in a saucepan with the water and heat gently until dissolved. Bring to the boil and boil until the temperature reaches 225°F (110°C) on a sugar thermometer. Beat the egg yolks in a bowl until pale. Pour the syrup in a thin stream on to the egg yolks, whisking all the time. Continue to whisk until the mixture is thick and cold. Beat the butter until light and fluffy. Gradually beat the egg mixture into the butter until evenly blended. Spread over the cupcakes immediately.

TIP

You could also flavor this with cold strong coffee for use on coffee and walnut cupcakes.

Praline

This is a simple decoration that looks pretty on an iced cupcake.

¾ cup unbalanced whole almonds
½ cup granulated sugar

Place the almonds and sugar into a saucepan over a very low heat. Stir continually until the nuts are toasted and the sugar has caramelized to a rich golden color. Lightly grease a cookie sheet. Carefully pour the praline over the sheet. Leave until completely cold, then break into pieces, pound with a rolling pin or blitz to a finer texture in a food processor. Store in an airtight container.

TIP

Hazelnut praline is also easy to make and tastes great—use one part hazelnuts to one part sugar.

Caramel Shards

This is a strong sugar syrup which needs to be boiled to a golden caramel color. If it's not boiled enough the caramel won't set; boiled too much and it will burn.

½ cup superfine or granulated sugar
3 tbsp. water

Dissolve the sugar in the water in a saucepan over a gentle heat. Bring to the boil and boil to a golden caramel. Oil or line a baking sheet with parchment paper. Pour over the caramel and leave until set hard. Break into small pieces. Use within one day.

Lemon Curd

This goes really well spooned over hot cupcakes. For different flavor curds, replace the lemon with the same quantity of orange zest and juice or passion fruit pulp.

1 cup granulated sugar
¼ cup cornstarch
⅛ tsp. salt
1¼ cups warm water
¼ cup fresh lemon juice

zest from 1 lemon
3 large egg yolks,
lightly beaten
1 tbsp. unsalted butter

Combine the granulated sugar, cornstarch, and salt in a double boiler. Over low heat, slowly whisk in the warm water. Then add the lemon juice and zest, egg yolks, and butter. Cook, whisking constantly, until the mixture comes to a boil and thickens. The lemon curd should mound when dropped from a spoon. Remove from the heat.

TIP

For different flavor curds, replace the lemon with the same quantity of orange zest and juice or passion fruit pulp. This lemon curd recipe is used in the Lemon Meringue Cupcakes, page 22.

Vanilla Custard

This custard goes perfectly with the Mixed Berry Crumble cupcakes (page 218).

2½ cups milk
1 tsp. vanilla extract
¼ cup superfine sugar
8 large egg yolks

Heat the milk in a saucepan until almost boiling. Stir in the vanilla extract and leave to cool slightly. Beat together the sugar and egg yolks in a large bowl with an electric mixer until thick, about 3 minutes. Whisk in the cooled milk mixture and return the mixture to the saucepan. Cook the sauce, stirring constantly, until it begins to thicken and coats the back of a wooden spoon. Strain into a bowl and serve immediately or cool and refrigerate for up to 1 day.

TIP

Take care not to boil as it will curdle.

Caramel Toffee Sauce

This sauce goes well with any fruity cupcake.

10 tbsp. granulated sugar
4 tbsp. water
8 tbsp. heavy cream

Put the sugar into a saucepan with the water. Cook over a low heat until the sugar dissolves. Boil until a golden caramel forms. Remove from the heat and add the cream. Stir until melted and smooth.

TIP

Be extra careful while you are cooking the sugar. Once the sugar has melted it has a much higher temperature than boiling water. Also, when you add the cream, the mixture will foam up, so use a pan with high sides.

Index of Recipes

Index of Ingredients

Note: The following ingredients have not been indexed, as they each occur in the great majority of the recipes: baking powder, butter, eggs, flour, sugar, vanilla extract.

Picture Credits

A = above, B = below, C=center, L=left, R=right

All other images are the copyright of Quintet Publishing Ltd. While every effort has been made to credit contributors, Quintet Publishing would like to apologize should there have been any omissions or errors—and would be pleased to make the appropriate correction for future editions of the book.